MW01141135

# So, What'll You Have, Do or Be, Hon?

**Living Your Truth,
Loving Yourself,
Changing Your Life and the World**

Monika Huppertz

To Dianne
Thanks so much
for your support.

---

A gift for

With love and
gratitude.

Monika

---

From

# So,
# What'll You
# Have, Do or Be,
# Hon?

**Living Your Truth,
Loving Yourself,
Changing Your Life and the World**

Monika Huppertz

Copyright © 2010 by Monika Huppertz.

ISBN:         Hardcover         978-1-4500-8609-7
              Softcover         978-1-4500-8532-8

All rights reserved. No part of this book may be reproduced or transmitted in any form or by any means, electronic or mechanical, including photocopying, recording, or by any information storage and retrieval system, without permission in writing from the copyright owner.

The intent of the author is to offer information of a general nature to help you in your quest for emotional and spiritual wellbeing. The material is designed to provide useful advice in regard to the subject matter covered. In the event that you use any of this information for yourself, which is your constitutional right, the author and the publisher assume no responsibility for your actions. The author and publisher expressly disclaim any responsibility for any liability, loss or risk, personal or otherwise, that is incurred as a consequence, directly or indirectly of the use and application of any of the contents of this book.

Readers should be aware that internet web sites listed in this work may have changed or disappeared between when this work was written and when it is read.

*www.livingyourtruth.me*
*www.lightheart.me*

This book was printed in the United States of America.

**To order additional copies of this book, contact:**
Xlibris Corporation
1-888-795-4274
www.Xlibris.com
Orders@Xlibris.com
64543

# Table of Contents

My inspiration:

God, Love, Universe, I trust you.
If this I what I am meant to do, then please work through me;
Use me as a vehicle to express yourself to the world.

**Dedicated to those searching for truth:**

**This is a good start.**

My dharma* is to spread God's work and word
through teaching others.
This is the answer to my "why".
What is yours?
Monika

*Dharma: in Buddhism, the truth about the way things are, and will always be, in the
universe or in nature, especially when contained in scripture. ~ Encarta Dictionary;
English (North America)

*Throughout *Indian philosophy*, Dharma is presented as a central concept that is
used in order to explain the "higher truth" or ultimate reality of the universe. The
word *dharma* literally translates as *that which upholds or supports*, and is generally
translated into English as *law*. The word "dharma" can also be translated as "the
teachings of the Buddha". ~ Wikipedia On-Line Dictionary

# Review

Monika brings to life in her book a modern parable that brings the concept of ease and joy into my life. I found it to be an easy read and deeply transformational. While reading "*So, What'll You Have, Do or Be, Hon?—Living Your Truth, Loving Yourself, Changing Your Life and the World*" I could see a number of my students and friends who could benefit by Monika's transformational parable.

Tim Summers,
Edmonton, Alberta, Canada

# Acknowledgements

I'd like to thank and acknowledge:

Chris and Ollie Huppertz, for their support and encouragement in all ways.

Megan Kelley, for her belief in me and my work.

Tim Summers, whose love, friendship and gentle nudging put this material into circulation.

Lisa Wojna and Penny Stanley, whose editing skills found the essence in my book and made sure that others were able to do so as well.

Friends, family and other supporters whose suggestions, comments and encouragement aided in the final processes of this book's creation.

Kelsey and Katie, for just being.

Charlie, for his comical antics.  =^..^=

And to those beings and entities whose words and concepts were channeled to this author to be brought into publication form.

In loving memory of Kelsey and Katie.

*"The greatest tragedy is not death, but life without purpose."* ~ Rick Warren

"**Life is an opportunity, benefit from it.**
**Life is beauty, admire it.**
**Life is bliss, taste it.**
**Life is a dream, realize it.**
**Life is a challenge, meet it.**
**Life is a duty, complete it.**
**Life is a game, play it.**
**Life is a promise, fulfill it.**
**Life is sorrow, overcome it.**
**Life is a song, sing it.**
**Life is a struggle, accept it. Life is a tragedy, confront it.**
**Life is an adventure, dare it.**
**Life is luck, make it.**
**Life is too precious, do not destroy it.**
**Life is life, fight for it.**"
~ Mother Teresa

*"I have come to the frightening conclusion that I am
the decisive element.
It is my personal approach that creates the climate. It is my daily
mood that makes the weather.
I possess tremendous power to make life miserable or joyous.
I can be a tool of torture or an instrument of inspiration; I can
humiliate or humor, hurt or heal. In all situations, it is my response
that decides whether a crisis is escalated or deescalated, and a person
is humanized or de-humanized.
If we treat people as they are, we make them worse.
If we treat people as they ought to be, we help them become
what they are capable of becoming."
~ Goethe*

**Things may come to those who wait
but only the things left by those who hustle.**
~ Abraham Lincoln

# Introduction

Have you decided to gain a higher state of awareness and consciousness? Do you seek answers to your *why*? Are you looking for a beginning to your path to understanding why life is not going as you had hoped and desired? Are you looking for a change?

Yes? Great! This means you are ready to do something about your life! You are here because you wish to start taking steps toward living your truth. Hooray!

You will look at clearing your fear and then figure out what is wanted and desired. Then you can take some small consistent inspired actions towards manifesting. You will soon be living your dreams and rejoicing in your accomplishments!

Read and enjoy making your life a dream come true. Start to shift and you will see everything in a new light. Guaranteed!

Did you think: "But am I really ready?"

The very fact that you are seeking this knowledge proves that you are *wanting* to and are *ready* to live a fulfilling life. This information will consistently find its way to all those who are prepared to live a different life than before. It was no accident that you found this book. There are no "accidents."

Uncertain, timid, shy, scared? Of course; but also hopeful, optimistic, eager and energized! Being ready doesn't mean without any fear or trepidation. You can be ready to live a life that you deserve and still feel hesitant, unworthy, or unsure of change. It's natural to feel a little bit scared moving from the familiar into the unknown. This is true even if what's familiar is uncomfortable, rough or painful.

*   *   *

It may surprise you to discover that even though people may want very much to change something, it still takes a lot of convincing to actually take the steps to move forward. If you think about it, you'll probably remember a time or two that you've had some difficulty making something stick despite all of your wanting, intentions or actions. Here is one memory of mine.

As a child in elementary school, I didn't really care for reading. I could read, but I read each word and each syllable, sounding out the letters in my head just before saying them out loud. I remember going to a remedial teacher for a period of time during the school day and practicing to read faster.

By junior high, I still didn't enjoy this arduous task. I recall losing my smile and lamenting getting books for birthday presents instead of craft kits and art supplies. I spent a lot of time both wishing I could read well and hoping that the teacher would not call on me to read aloud. That is, until one day, I had a teacher who spoke frankly to me about this problem. She explained to me that the only way I was going to become good at reading was to read, read, read and read some more. She explained that it was the best, quickest, most effective and definite way I was going to have my dream come true.

This teacher took the time to explain to me *why*. *Why* is it important to read well? To be informed. *Why* should I learn to read smoothly? To get the meaning of the message—the gift of the words on the paper. *Why* do I want that gift? To experience the beauty, the truth, the answers and the poetry that words can provide. Oh. Okay. Now I get it! Thanks. So I seriously thought about why I should put in time and effort into this endeavor.

While getting some books from the school's library, I was assisted by a lovely young woman. I really appreciated all the time and energy she spent on me to get the right materials for a project I had to do for one of my classes. This lady had a positive impact on me; so much so that I found myself asking if she needed any help around the library.

I helped out in the school library on a regular basis and came to know our wonderful librarian, Mrs. S. Foster. She loved books and that love shone through her. She was a kind and gentle soul that I wanted to emulate, so I thought some more about why I should spend more of my time on improving my reading skills.

Then the oddest thing happened. I was watching a television show called *Get Smart*. I enjoyed the comical banter that went on between the agents of Control and Kaos. One episode in particular piqued my interest. Agent 86—Maxwell Smart, was interrogating a prisoner by firing off question after question. The poor fellow being peppered with this barrage had barely enough time to respond when another question was fired at him. Finally Agent 86 got right up in his face and asked, "Who wrote *Little Women*?" The person he was interrogating didn't know the answer.

For some reason, I *had* to find out the answer to that question. I asked my folks and they had no idea. I asked the librarian and she retrieved a book from the shelf and presented it to me. It was a paperback novel that was 30 centimetres thick! Well, maybe seven centimetres thick, but the print was quite small! So, I figured, if it was important enough for Maxwell Smart to ask, it was important enough for Monika to answer.

And that was it. I was hooked. I read, read, read, read, read. I could not get enough. Some people may remember how the Harry Potter and Goose Bumps book series were catalysts for children, teens and young adults alike to read like never before. For me, it was the trials, tribulations and escapades of Jo March. Her spirit and love of life captivated my heart and my attention. I read during supper and I read aloud in class. I read in my bedroom. When my mother told me to go outside and get some sun on my face, I took my book outside and read there.

It was not uncommon now for me to be reading several books at once, yet still knowing what was happening in each one and being able to discuss possible future plots! I became a reading machine. I loved getting books for birthday presents now. In fact, I preferred it! *Nancy Drew, Hardy Boys* (which I wouldn't admit to reading as they were considered to be *boys'* books), some classics, some *Harlequin Romance* novels, *Archie* comics and hard covered books all found their way to the bookshelves in my room.

My *why* of "*Why* should I read?" was answered sufficiently enough to give me the freedom to explore and in doing so, I became enlightened. Taking on the responsibility of learning to read well, freed me from the drudgery, dread and embarrassment of reading poorly. By the way, the person who wrote *Little Women* was Louisa May Alcott.

*     *     *

Now it is your turn. Find the answer to your *why*. Perhaps the answer lies in the pages of this book; if not this book, perhaps another or a video, or a television show, or a song or a friend or even within. Rekindle the feeling of wonder and possibility.

Make a decisive decision today to think past your fears, your past and your negative unsupportive conditioning. Make a decisive decision today to dream, plan, think, feel and take action. You won't regret what ever you do; you'll only regret what ever you don't do.

Find your truth and then act upon it. Whether you view the world from a scientific point of view, a spiritual perspective, a Christian viewpoint, an ecumenical perception or an atheist position, Truth is Truth. Why would you wait? Do you feel you have a long life ahead of you before you have to take some form of action? Perhaps you are waiting for more life experiences to come your way before you'll feel the need to decide to take matters into your own hands? Hmmm? What is it?

Think about it this way, if you take just one small step today by reading this or any other self-enlightening material, you have already begun that journey. It's that simple. You asked for information and assistance and found motivation and guidance placed in your hands. Now, are you going to use it?

Understand this; take care of yourself first and the whole world will benefit. Yes, really. The world can not receive your gifts until you make a definite decision and act upon it. Once you *act* on your decision, energy, Spirit and the Universe will immediately start a chain of events. It will move you towards the situations, people and resources you require to make that dream manifest.

Honour yourself and your own experiences. Stay true to yourself and the integrity that is you. Be willing to take a risk and be adventuresome. There is a wonderful adventure out there for you to enjoy and partake in. Utilize the information contained within this publication as a starting point for your journey. Trust your intuition, use what fits and feels right and put aside what does not grab your attention. You can always relook at that information at some later date if you find yourself seeking a different vantage point or to understand a newly discovered truth.

So take a leap of faith and soar to new heights. After all, a LEAP is

**L**oving
**E**nergy
**A**pplied
**P**urposefully.

Start a *change* reaction in your life.

Express what you have bottled up inside of you.

We need you!

Hugs,
Monika
☺

= ^ .. ^ =

# One

## Universal Delights

It had been a long day, even though this day was no longer than the usual 24 hours. Kelly felt as though time had ticked by particularly slow today. As she walked out of her office building her mind was preoccupied with thoughts of wishing for some sort of change. *Wouldn't it be nice if something different happened today? I'm tired of the same old same old. I'd love to, just for once, experience something new.*

Her body, reflecting the drudgery of her day, was a little stooped; her shoulders slumped. Faced with the problem of what to have for supper, she spied the erratic flashing neon sign of a diner down the road. As it flashed dine . . . dine . . . diner . . . dine . . . diner, the lights beckoned to her, offering a solution to her meal-for-one in her empty apartment. She headed toward the diner with a sense of relief, having dealt with the subject of supper.

As Kelly entered, she noticed the woman standing behind the counter waiting to take her order. She appeared to be rather tall, plump, and in her 50s. She wore a traditional white waitress uniform, apron and matching white cap. The woman wore horn-rimmed glasses and a great big smile. Her eyes sparkled and she had a certain presence in her stance that said "I am comfortable with who I am. I like me. I like my job. I like you." This waitress seemed unusual and different. She was unlike anyone Kelly had ever remembered meeting before. Yet there was a most welcoming feeling emanating from her which helped to melt away some of the day's stressors.

"What'll you have, do or be, Hon?" Looking down at the menu, Kelly was trying to quickly make a decision. Feeling flustered and self-conscious about taking so much time to decide, Kelly blurted "I'll have the usual."

"Oh," says the waitress, "You don't really want any of that, Dear. It's stale and chalky and does nothing to serve what you really desire." Stunned, perplexed and a little amused, Kelly looked up at the face of the lady behind the counter. A warm smile greeted her gaze. "Wouldn't it be nice if you ordered something different today? Aren't you tired of the same old, same old? Wouldn't you love, just for once, to experience something new?"

"Yes," Kelly heard herself say, "What would you recommend?"

"Well," says the waitress, "There are many choices that you could make. Let's see, here. There is a delicious bowl of Love and Kindness. The Dance Like No One is Looking is nice. Oh, there's also the Letting Go of the Old So That There's Room For The New to Come In, appetizer. However, in your case, I'm going to suggest the Success Platter. It's full of self love, you know!"

Kelly blinked her eyes and stared with bewilderment at the order taker. Was she just trying to be funny? She sure had a different sense of humour if that was the case. Once again, feeling the self imposed pressure of taking up too much time, Kelly agreed to the Success Platter and prepared to step aside so that the next person could place their order. There was quite a line up behind her now and she didn't want to cause a scene.

Reaching for her purse, Kelly was about to take some money out of her wallet when she heard the waitress say, "Sweetie, you don't pay me. Once you ask for guidance and decide what you want, the next step is to take some action towards getting your order fulfilled. Go to the next counter to pick up the things that you'll need. It's right over there." The woman pointed to a place behind Kelly. Looking to see her next destination, Kelly turned back to thank the woman. The waitress was already dealing with the next customer so Kelly proceeded to the next counter as instructed. The waitress looked up and watched to see that Kelly made it successfully to her next destination.

At the counter, a short, round gruff looking man was busily putting things in order. Kelly waited for him to notice her. He didn't and she grew impatient. Finding herself with no other choice but to speak up, Kelly said in a rather firm tone, "Excuse me. I ordered the Success Platter." The man turned to face her. His eyes were warm and tender. The look that he gave Kelly melted away any chill she had felt. Kelly felt a little guilty and embarrassed to have spoken the way that she did, but the man did not seem upset at all. In fact, he stopped what he was doing and gave her his full attention. Fumbling for her wallet yet again, she asked how much the platter was going to cost.

A soothing deep voice came from the face of the little round man. "I'm glad you spoke up, Miss. I get so caught up in what I'm doing, that unless someone takes the initiative to get my attention, I'm afraid that I just don't notice them. Thank you for having the courage to inform me of your desire. My appearance may seem a little scary to some, but I assure you that I don't bite. Well, not hard anyway." His smile and the glint in his eye matched the smile and amusement on her face. "There's no charge for the Success Platter, Miss. After you've had it and only if you liked the outcome, you are welcome to spread a kind word our way. That's payment enough for us. Hey, since it will take a bit of time before your order is ready, can I get you a beverage of some sort?"

"Umm, yes please. Green tea would be nice."

"One green tea, coming right up, miss. Cream, sugar, lemon and honey are at the end of the counter. Please help yourself. I'll call you when your order is ready, okay? In the meantime, find a nice seat by the window. There are books and magazines to peruse while you wait. If you should change your mind, I'll change the order right away. Your wish is my command. Okay?"

"Umm, okay. Thank you."

"You are most welcome, Miss." As she walked away, unbeknownst to her, the busy man kept his eye on her while he went about his business.

Kelly chose a table by the window. There was a bookshelf near by. One book in particular caught her eye. It was one that she had read before. *Conversations with God* was the title. She recalled that her father had lent Neale Donald Walsch's first book to her a while ago. The uplifting feeling she had while reading that story filled her mind for a moment. That hard cover novel appeared at a time when she needed to take a new direction in her life. Well, life went on, a little better than before and soon Kelly forgot all about the white book with the painting on the cover. Remembering now brought a soft smile to her lips and a glow to her heart.

On the table was a case that held some magazines. *Entrepreneur, Time, Millionaire Blueprint, People, Life, Cosmopolitan*, the good old *Reader's Digest* and one that she usually bought when she was feeling down, Oprah Winfrey's magazine—*O*. As she mindlessly thumbed through *O*, she recalled something that Oprah had once said; *"You are responsible for your life. You can't keep blaming somebody else for your dysfunction. Life is really about moving on."* A song playing on the speakers caught her attention. It was by that young fellow, Josh Groban. *"Don't give up . . . because you are loved . . . ."* What a lovely tune to hear right now.

Taking a sip of her tea, she wondered whether her order was ready yet. A look over told her that it was not. A feeling of concern and doubt came to mind.

The woman and the man behind the counters looked up from their tasks and looked towards her.

What if the waitress forgot to put the order through?

The eyes behind the horned-rimmed glasses looked concerned.

What if the man got so busy that her order was either forgotten or misplaced?

The little man turned his ear towards Kelly as if he was trying to hear what she was thinking.

Nah, she thought, of course it will come. Why would it not? She had placed the order and it will come when it is the perfect time to arrive. What is that called? Divine timing? Something like that.

Smiles appeared on the faces of both of the counter people as they happily resumed their tasks.

Along with the magazines was a detailed menu from the restaurant, Universal Delights. Kelly picked it up and saw a picture of her choice on the first page. In fact, the Success Platter was the very first item on the menu. There were all sorts of delightful goodies in her order. Fresh, wholesome ingredients, some raw foods added in for energy and nutrients, and cold crab claws. All were made with love and served on a down to earth whole grain bun-loaf, with dessert, too.

Some of the items would need a few tools in order to get through the tough outer shell; but since she already had the necessary utensils for the job, there was really no need to be concerned. A little effort would be worth it in order to be rewarded with the wonderful prize inside. Sometimes there is just as much fun in the doing as there is in the having.

Someone walking by the window caught her eye. A boy with a hockey stick and a pair of skates slung over the blade was practically skipping as he headed in the direction of the ice rink near by. Kelly remembered how much her little brother loved the game. Hockey was all that he ate, drank and breathed, or so it seemed. He never went anywhere without that stick of his. At night he would dream of being a great hockey player, like Wayne Gretzsky or Guy Lafleur. During the day he would share his dreams of scoring goals and winning games. After hockey practice, he would sometimes tell of the frustration of not being put in—he didn't want to just dream about being a hockey player; there was little reward in that. He wanted to *have* the experience, *do* the drills and practices and *be* on the ice. He wanted to get into the game because that was what he loved to do. Taking action is what made Steve the happiest, not the dreaming, not the bragging, not the remembering; it was the doing.

Ah, the exuberance of youth. If it were not for the accident that prevented him from entering into the pros, he would have been a great player, indeed. But the game did not die inside of Steve. Now a happily married man with kids of his own, he coaches the minors and still enjoys the thrill of the game. Steve always did have things go his way. Even when they didn't, it was only a matter of a short time before he was back on his feet again, wearing that happy grin of his. Mr. Sunshine they used to call him. In fact, some of the uncles on Mom's side of the family still do.

Now something else caught her attention; a sound. Did she imagine it? She looked up and saw that the guy at the counter had just placed down her order. I guess they just don't go and hand it to you on a silver platter around here, she grinned. As she crossed the room, she caught his eye and nodded a thank you for the meal. A great big smile met her and a returned nod of you're welcome was given. Both went about their business with a smile and a sense of satisfaction.

When she sat at the table, Kelly removed the dishes on the tray to the table's surface. Under her order was a little book. The title was intriguing;

*Love of Self—Steps to Your Success.*

Scribbled on the cover page was a hand written note:

With my compliments—G.
P. S. Enjoy!

Kelly began to eat her delicious meal and casually flipped through the little book. Several headings caught her attention. "What Do You Wish You Were Doing Right Now?; Do You Know What Makes You Happy?; There Is a Powerful Force Within You; Are You Happy Just Sitting on The Curb?; This Little Light of Mine—I'm Gonna Let it Shine!; and Set Your Sights: Aim High and Smile!" The light was beginning to fade and Kelly thought she had better be getting home. She really did not like being in the dark. She felt scared and uneasy when she had to walk home alone especially when the light was fading. A take out container for the hard shelled items and her desert was procured and Kelly made her way back to her condo, containers and the little book in tow.

Once home, a feeling of suffocating safety entered her body. She put the containers in the fridge and the new book on the coffee table. Charlie, her cat, was waiting for his dinner. "Meow?" "Hi Charlie, how's a pussy cat?" Kelly petted the long-haired cat. Arching his back to get more out of the petting, "Purr," was his response. As she proceeded to her bedroom to get out of her business attire and into some comfortable casual duds, Charlie raced by and jumped up onto the bed. "Meow?" "Yes Charlie, I'll be there for you in a moment. "Meooooowwwwwww!" "I said, yes, Charlie, just a minute, please. "Meow!" "Oy!—you just don't give up until you get what you want, do you?" "Errrr. Meow?" "I'm coming, let me put my pants on." "Meow!" A long white paw was gently extended towards her as she faced the persistent creature. "Is your staff not taking proper care of you? Boy oh boy! Come on, Handsome, let's see what you need." "Meow—purr!" "How may I serve you, your majesty? Ask so that I may grant your deepest wishes and desires." "Meow!" "Your wish is my command. I am forever your most humble of servants," said Kelly laughingly, as she bowed toward the cat.

As she made her way back to the kitchen, Charlie skipped past her and waited for his favourite staff to put down his food next to his water dish. Feeling a little devilish, she ducked into the bathroom behind the door and waited; a sly grin growing across her face. It didn't take long for the cat to find her and make his requests known once more. "Meow?" "Okay there my pussy cat. I'm coming. I was only teasing you, you know." "Meow!"

Kelly thought of her brother once again as she passed by his picture in the hall. Charlie had something in common with Steve, alright. They both pursued their goals until they achieved them. If something derailed them, they simply made the necessary corrections to put their targets back into sight and continued. If they were told no, or something did not go their way at that time, that was okay. They were not attached to the outcome being achieved by a particular time. They simply resumed their activity with even more conviction the next time.

"Meow?" "Soft or crunchy today, Sir?" "Meow!" "I believe that means crunchy." "Erneow! Purr." "You sure know the secret to manifesting what you want, don't ya, boy? You always seem to manage to attract it somehow. I wish that I had the same results that you and Steve have." A noisy crunch of the hard kibble was the only reply to her comment.

"Cats!" said Kelly, as she left the kitchen and walked into the living room. Plunking herself onto the couch, Kelly scrolled through the TV channels. Too late for Oprah, she thought. Sigh. Same old, same old . . . News . . . Dead guy . . . Woman being stalked . . . Oh, there we go, axe in the head . . . Raymond . . . Ellen . . . She held at that station for a minute. Ellen DeGeneres was dancing. Kelly enjoyed Ellen's show. She loved the comedian's style. Charming and warm, like a favourite pair of jeans that fit right, look good and feel good.

"Every channel had its own frequency. What was it that they were talking about at work about frequencies? Energy made up things and those things each resonated at a different frequency, just a like a television station. Hmm. Maybe I did learn something new today," thought Kelly.

Speaking of new . . . Kelly looked at the book on the coffee table. Perhaps a little light reading would be a better way to kill some time. She picked up the book and sat up a little more on the couch. What else was there to do?

# Two

## Self Love and Success

*Love of Self—Step Towards Your Success*
Chapter 1 Definition of Success

What is success? The *Encarta Dictionary* defines success, a noun, with the following meanings:

1. Achievement of desired aim—the achievement of something planned or attempted.
2. Attainment of fame, wealth or power—impressive achievement, especially the attainment of fame, wealth or power.
3. Something that turns out well—something that turns out as planned or intended.
4. Somebody who has significant achievements—somebody who has a record of achievement, especially in gaining wealth, fame or power.

What does success mean to you? To some people, success is indicated by fitting nicely into society; to others, being able to precisely carry out orders or instructions. Most people would agree with the dictionary's definition, but then again, are these the only ways to define success?

What does success mean to me? I further define success as being brave enough to follow what my heart, intuition and what

Spirit urges me to do. To take a stand and face what ever comes my way, takes courage. Connecting to the heart and to Spirit means being in the realm of endless positive possibilities, a place where I am guided in the direction of happiness, joy and true fulfilment. It is in the ability and opportunity to express myself that leads directly to my success, my happiness and what brings me joy. It honours my feelings. In fact, I would further say that the meaning of success to me is, when I love myself enough to stand up for what I believe in and am willing to take the steps to fruition of that belief. Sustained fulfilment for me has never come from grudgingly giving into society's pressures and persuasions, nor to limiting my ability to freely communicate what is welling up inside of me, waiting to be expressed. I want to be true to myself. I love myself enough to know that much.

Love myself? Self love? What a narcissistic way of thinking! Actually no, it's not. The narcissistic statement is a reflection of a negative non-loving belief. I'll tell you *why* it is important to *love yourself* . . . . why loving yourself is the prime ingredient to your *success*: Honouring your feelings, your heart's desires and what you really want to do . . .honour your Spirit's calling. Honouring what your Spirit wants makes you successful in your life. In fact, it is the only true way to make you successful and sustain that triumph.

When questioned to pinpoint the most important asset of anything a person has when being interviewed for life insurance, investments or business opportunities, many people would confidently answer my health, my family or my job. Imagine the look on their faces when they hear the questioner say that although all of those things are very important, the true answer is y-o-u, you.

Without you, there is nothing else to discuss. There is no one to insure, no one to bring in your salary, nothing else; period. When studies have been conducted and the wealthy and accomplished participants were queried to list the top three reasons for their success, the number one answer was always "myself." Without them, the success that they achieved would not have been expressed in the same manner as it has been. Family, friends and even God were tied for second and third place spots, but these people *recognized that they themselves were the main ingredient in their own success.*

With that being said, would it not make sense then to look after and nurture your greatest asset? Perhaps even love it? I put it to you that not only does it make perfect sense to love yourself but even further, it also makes sense to honour and value yourself as well. A healthy love of self will get you where you want to go and *is* the key to your success.

Have you ever noticed that when people value and love themselves enough to listen to their heart and their Spirit they always seem to be moving in the direction of happily fulfilling their goals and dreams? Not only that but often, if not always, they are doing jobs and things that serve the needs of others. Think about it. Doing what they love is a "selfish" act that serves society at large.

Consider a cab driver who patiently listens to your story as you travel to your destination. Not only has he managed to get you swiftly and safely across town and to the airport on time, but the time just flew by as you enjoyed the ride, the conversation and were gifted with some pearls of wisdom to boot!

I love it when I come across people who are happy in their occupations. How about the musician who lives for his music and expresses himself in that medium? He touches the lives of many others through his songs, melodies, music and lyrics. Who here has not been feeling down one time or another and then, out of the blue, a song is played and you found yourself in a better mood? It lifted your spirits! Sometimes I swear that a particular song was written just for me. The words spoke to my heart and I felt renewed.

What about the teacher who listens to the little girl as she explains why staying in for recess to avoid a bully is a great reason why she should be instead allowed to help out in the classroom. The teacher recognises that it is not in the little girl's best interest to be bullied and neither is it in the bully's best interest to keep on bullying. So, the teacher ensures that she talks to the bully to see what his true needs are and deals with the situation as best as can be. Later, the little girl discovers that the bullying problem has been solved and she happily skips home instead of having to dash to safety in fear and in tears.

As a parent, I would be truly grateful that my little one was listened to, valued and heard, and that actions were taken to ensure a happy outcome. I would also be happy that someone spoke to my child to stop a behaviour that was self-damaging. Interestingly enough, teachers are rarely appreciated for giving their time and doing the right thing for all concerned. Most teachers just give naturally. Their reward is in the smile of the little ones who happily go about their day being themselves, doing what brings them joy, having a wonderful experience.

Even business people who love what they are doing serve other people through their services and products. I know there are many items that I own that I would not be without and am grateful for those people's dedication and ingenuity being expressed and manifested into form. When these people "selfishly" considered listening to their heart's desires and were brave enough to take the steps to *have*, *do* and *be* what they wanted in life, they ended up being successful. They also served society at large as well.

It is so very important to listen to your heart's desires so that the Universal Spirit can express Itself through you. It is a journey of emotion that is very easy to know and understand when it is being accomplished. How? By simply recognizing your own feelings, you will know instantly if you're on the right track. If you are feeling happy, joyful, satisfied, excited with life and have a plan or goal in mind to achieve, then you are on the right track. If you are bored, angry, sad, anxious and fearful or are anything else that does not bring you good feelings, then there is an issue to address and actions to take, to bring about a rewarding desired outcome.

Let's face it, when given a choice, who would choose to be sad, miserable, lonely and lacking? You could just as easily make the choice to be happy, joyful, in good company and have abundance in all things good. It's an emotional journey, to be sure. I know what choice I would make, most of the time.

When I'm not aware that there is a choice to be made, it may take the kindness of others to show me a different option, to help me to remember and realize that I have a choice. Friends, family, associates, books, songs and movies can each offer that kindness. I am then able to make a conscious and more fully informed decision.

*"Oh, I get by with a little help from my friends." ~ Beatles*

\*    \*    \*

Kelly pondered the first chapter of her new book. The idea of self-love was not one that she had felt comfortable with. It was, to her, an issue of the ego and not one that Kelly wanted to delve into. Yet, the way that it was explained here made sense to her; it resonated with her own truth.

Hmm, she thought; it seemed that self love was as good a starting place as any to gain a little self confidence and to experience joy and happiness. Life is too precious for regrets to be the main thing to think about in old age or upon a death bed. It would be much more pleasant to enjoy one's accomplishments and relive fond and happy memories of the victories that made life worth living when it came her time to leave.

Kelly stopped and pondered what expressing love to herself would look like. An amusing picture came to her mind. She was looking at a photograph of herself in a heart shaped frame. On the picture was handwritten an "autograph" reading,

To Kelly,
With all my love,
Kelly.

She grinned at the thought of such a scene. It felt good to *feel* that love from herself. In the photo, the look on her face was one of adoration. To see love, adoration, admiration and acceptance in her own eyes for herself, took Kelly a bit aback. Yet there was no denying what that wonderful feeling of love . . . unconditional love . . . did to her. She liked the feeling. She liked the feeling a lot!

With the "mutual admiration society" episode over, an amused and cheeky feeling Kelly resumed reading the little book once more.

# Three

## Love and Light

*Love of Self—Step Towards Your Success*
Chapter 2 This Little Light of Mine—I'm Gonna Let it Shine!

'Love thy neighbour as thyself." Did you know that loving someone, including yourself, is a *decision* you make? Love thy neighbour as thyself? This means not to love your neighbour in spite of yourself or instead of yourself, but as if the neighbour was yourself. This also means that in order for a person to give of himself (love thy neighbour), first and foremost, that person must have love (as thyself) to begin with.

You are not able to give that which you don't *feel* or don't *think* you do not have to begin with. But you *do* have love inside; all of you have love to give. The love and abundance in a person *is* there to be expressed and shared with others. People want to love, express love and experience love from others. To connect with others is programmed within you. It is a natural instinct to join or bond with others, just as it is to want to feel appreciated for what you give or share. You are part of a collective, from one source, manifested as individuals who seek to experience who and what you are.

People impact each other whether they consciously know it or not. Remember that we are all one. There have been many books written on this subject in recent years. They all mention that we come from one source of energy and that like ripples in a pond, what you do does indeed make some sort of impact on the rest. We are interconnected with one another, sort of like being part of a matrix or a web. When a vibration is felt on one part of a spider's web, the whole thing vibrates to some degree or another.

Since we make a difference in one another's lives, it therefore makes sense to take care of you—love yourself, first. Remember, you have an abundant supply of love to give. You also have free will and choice and so you can choose to accept or reject love. Let your light shine so that you can light the way for others to find you and to facilitate others finding themselves in the process.

Love is not about pleasing others; it is, however, about allowing your light and joy to radiate from inside out to the collective and to the Universe. It is in you to give. It always was and always will be. You have the choice to recognise and remember that, and use it, or refuse it. It is up to you to decide whether to share and thus love yourself, or not share and thus shield your light not only from others, but from yourself as well. In fact, your own success depends upon *your decision* whether to let it shine or not!

*"We can easily forgive a child who is afraid of the dark; the real tragedy is when men are afraid of the light." ~ Plato*

\*        \*        \*

"Ding dong." The door bell rang loud and clear and startled Kelly into jumping up off of the couch. It was her brother Steve's eye peering at her as she looked through the peep hole. Opening the door, Kelly soon found herself wrapped in her brother's arms. She could almost feel that grin of his beaming at her.

"Hi 'ya, Sis! How're you doing? I brought back your Corel dishes. Marla washed them up real good." Her brother said as he strode into the apartment and noisily clanked the dishes down on the kitchen counter. Charlie rushed past him after giving a little jump at the sound of the noise. Within moments he was back, rubbing up against the long legs of the noise maker. It would appear that humans are not the only animals that seek to connect with others, Kelly observed. Kelly liked it when Steve came over. She felt safe, less nervous and more relaxed when he was there. She smiled as she observed her brother scratch Charlie behind his ears and then pull gently on the cat's tail. Charlie just purred, enjoying every bit of the man's attention.

Seeing the connection between the two men in her life brought a fleeting thought of her beloved, Tim. It was a long time since her fiancé had passed away. How long has it been? It was the day before Valentine's Day. They were going to meet at the little bistro where they had become engaged. Wow, that was nearly seven years ago! The car crash on that icy road had claimed his life. Kelly walked around in a daze for weeks after the funeral. Eventually she had slowly returned to her normal life, but she never felt quite the same again. She considered how far she had come. It had taken an awful long time to get there. When he left this earth, it seemed that her confidence and sense of security left with him.

Steve's head was now in the refrigerator looking for something to drink. Finding a pitcher of iced tea, he closed the door and took out two glasses from the cupboard. Walking to the living room he called over his shoulder, "What's new?" Kelly followed him and sat down across from him, a bag of oatmeal chocolate chip cookies in her hands. Before she could answer, Steve had picked up the odd little book and asked, "What's this, Sis?"

"That? It's just something that was given to me today at that quirky restaurant, Universal Delights. It's sort of interesting. I've only read the first two chapters so far, but it seems to be about love . . . . love of self, no, self-love is how it was put, connecting with others and how you impact one another, like ripples in a pond."

"Cool. I'll borrow it for Marla when you're finished, okay? She's been a reading fiend lately. Spiritual stuff, ya' know? What was that course she took? . . . *The Reconnection or Reconnective Healing (~ Eric Pearl)* . . . something like that. Anyway, she says she wants to keep up with the spiritual shifts and changes that are supposedly happening now and has probably read about 20 books in the last few months alone! She has three or four on the go all of the time lately. Love, patience, being non-judgemental and other such stuff is what we've been talking about. Hey . . . bonus . . . we've even been getting back that spark that we had when we first met. I guess what she does is having an effect on me. More ripples, I guess, eh?"

Steve grabbed the cookie out of Kelly's hand before she could take a bite and winked at her. After washing it down with a final swig of iced tea, he got up to go.

"Say hi to Marla and the kids for me, will you?" said Kelly.

"I'll give them your love," replied Steve as he kissed her on the forehead before heading out the door.

After locking the door, Kelly turned around and stood still listening to the deafening silence within her four walls.

Kelly sat back down on the couch and pondered the second chapter a little more. An old ditty that she learned in catechism class came to mind. Suddenly she started to softly sing the next verse. *"Hide it under a bush, oh no! I'm gonna let it shine . . . ."* She remembered how bold she felt when singing that song in class. Her friend Susan and her would always belt out the "oh no!" part with big smiles on their faces and a gleeful glint in their eyes. Kelly recalled feeling strong, uplifted and alive when singing that song. Maybe it would be a good mantra to use as she embarked on this journey.

"Hmm," thought Kelly, "Did I just consider following a new path?" Then she thought about her old friend. Susan was newly involved with a sweet man whom she met not too long ago and so the two had not been in touch lately. Maybe she should call her to catch up on the news and perhaps bounce some ideas off of Susan.

Nature was calling and so Kelly put down the book. Thoughts of Susan, the past and the new ideas filled her head while she took care of her needs.

As she walked back down the hall, she heard a rustling sound coming from the spare bedroom. Charlie was pouncing on his favourite cat nip mouse and had knocked over some CD cases onto the floor. As Kelly picked them up, she tossed the cat toy out into the hall sending Charlie scrambling after it, fur flying, as he hunted down his mobile prey. As she stood up, Kelly noticed that she had missed picking up a few of the CDs. *Pepper Lewis and the Peaceful Planet* were the words that she read on the little disks. Her spiritual mentor Lionel had told her about this lovely lady and the sentience, Gaia, which she channeled.

Some of Gaia's words from the CDs came to mind. *"What you must do is make the decision; I choose . . . , I have decided . . . , I am alive and will take a step and then course correct, take another step and course correct . . . , great beings are at your side ready to assist you . . . , take a risk and life will reward you. Become accustomed to receiving guidance from your whole Self—draw a communication with Self and trust your Self. Don't allow the gum that makes you stick act as if it is cement as it is not."*

Funny what a person recalls at times; Gaia's words had captured her full attention but at the time, did not inspire her to take action. Yet, there was an interesting feeling associated with remembering those words at this time. Wasn't it Gaia who had said something about people being given pertinent information? It was up to each person to use that information at the appropriate time, even if that time was days, weeks, months or sometimes years from the time of receiving that enlightenment. Kelly thought she'd listen to that CD once more; this time with new ears to hear the Truth that Gaia spoke.

Kelly sauntered back to the living room to read some more. As she passed the catnip mouse, she gave it a kick into the kitchen. From out of nowhere, Charlie came a running in hot pursuit, giving Kelly yet another reason to smile.

# Four

# Free Will and Choice

*Love of Self—Step Towards Your Success*
Chapter 3 What Do You Wish You Were Doing Right Now?

Stop for a moment and think about your life as it is currently. You *have* some things, you are *doing* some things and you are *being* some things. Most of this came about as a result of your thoughts, ideas, words, attitudes, beliefs, actions and expectations. People are very capable of acquisition. When people do something they love, they are in the *creative process* and life goes along quite smoothly, give or take a thing or two.

However, when people end up doing just about anything to make a buck for a living, they often find life more challenging and feel down-trodden. It could even feel as if they are prostituting themselves for money—doing something that they would rather not do, just to pay the bills.

Now consider this. The later group of people are unaware of how dire their circumstances are. They are so involved in the process of making money, that they can not see the forest for the trees, so to speak. Now, add some insight to the picture; someone says something to them, or they discover that there is something more to consider or their prayer *is* answered in the form of new information.

Finally, in their own time, this group begins to realize the importance of honouring their feelings and expressing love to others, and especially, expressing love to themselves. Before they know it, life begins to feel a little softer, a little kinder. They are inspired with new hope and optimism and begin the process of sharing their truth—their true selves with the rest of the world. The whole world benefits from their actions, from their light, from their courage.

Since you now know that following your heart and loving yourself will bring you happiness, is it so difficult to imagine that this too will bring the wealth that you all seek? Wealth, of course is not limited to simply money. Wealth means abundance. Many things such as love, time, friends, items and opportunistic circumstances increase. There are spiritual, mental, emotional and physical gains to be had. Now is the time to start taking steps in the direction that inspires and elates you. Now is the time to focus on what is desired and make manifest those desires.

All people are born with free will and choice. It is in your make up. In order to use your will you must first be made aware that there are options from which to choose. If, when you look and see only one thing, then there would appear to be only one thing to choose and thus, you take that which you feel is your only choice. When you are made aware of more options, then you are able to exercise your free will and make a choice that makes sense to you. Reverse polarity, as some call it, is a tool used for this very occasion. Simply stated, a list of negatives and positives will facilitate your free will to make choices that you were once unaware that you had. For example:

| Negatives | Positives |
|---|---|
| Takes too long | Benefits of having it in divine time |
| Uncle Paul says no | I am responsible for my own success |
| No money | Spirit will provide the providers—trust it |
| It's too hard—I'm not worthy | I'll grow and be better off as I *am* worthy |
| **Ending in failure** | **Ending in success** |

It is when you see and accept all possibilities that you are able to make a choice that, in your opinion, is the best for you, for your higher good, for your higher purpose as a form of self love or love of self. Whether you know it or not, you are invoking the Law of Attraction and being the creators that you truly are. You are able to manifest what you desire into your physical reality.

A person makes his or her own reality. Your circumstances were created by you. There's a saying that goes; if you can get *in* to it, you can get yourself *out* of it. Often it is through the very process of getting out of what a person gets into that changes a person, whether by self or facilitated through others, and often for the better. Just think of all the discoveries, choices, circumstances and events that were presented for the choosing. There is power in choice, freedom in choice, happiness in choice. Your circumstances were created by you, and now it is time for you to make a new choice so that your future will reflect that. What you focus on now will build your bright future.

\* \* \*

. . . . *Hide it under a bush, OH NO! I'm gonna let it shine; let it shine, let it shine, let it shine* . . . .

\* \* \*

Kelly put down the book and went to the phone. She pushed the speed dial button for Susan's number and heard the phone ring. "Hello?" said the familiar voice on the other end. "Susan? It's Kel. How are you?" Kelly and Susan chatted for a long while. Both women were happy to hear each other's voices and to reconnect once more. Susan shared the latest news about her new relationship. She sounded happy and content.

They giggled and laughed about men and choices and life. Kelly told her news about the little book from the diner. Susan listened intently. She asked several questions about what Kelly had read so far. Kelly shared her thoughts and opinions. She asked Susan for her opinion about free will and choice. Susan said that there was freedom in choice and staleness and lack when there is no perceived choice. Susan had also shared information about what a spirit may do after departing its physical body. According to her e-course, after they pass on, the spirit may choose to come back to Earth from time to time. Spirits will often come back to check up on their loved ones. "They like to stay connected to us," Susan said.

When she hung up, Kelly found herself feeling buoyant and upbeat. It felt good to laugh, think new thoughts and have her ideas heard and considered valid. "A win!" as Tim would say.

Kelly wondered if Tim was one of those great beings who were on her side, cheering her on. She concluded, that if such a thing as an afterlife did exist, that Tim would certainly be there, doing what he could to look after his 'little chickadee'. A warm smile crossed Kelly's lips. Thoughts of Tim came flooding into her mind; it was enjoyable to think of him this time; a nice change of pace; a win.

After a while, Kelly found her mind drifting back to the newly acquired book lying on her coffee table. Her eyes twinkled as she thought about what she had read.

*"It is so very important to listen to your heart's desires so that the Universal Spirit can express Itself through you. It is a journey of emotion that is very easy to know and understand when it is being accomplished. How? By simply recognizing your own feelings, you will know instantly if you're on the right track. If you are feeling happy, joyful, satisfied, excited with life and have a plan or goal in mind to achieve, then you are on the right track. If you are bored, angry, sad, anxious and fearful or are anything else that does not bring you good feelings, then there is an issue to address and actions to take, to bring about a rewarding desired outcome."*

Kelly wasn't sure if reading this book was her heart's desire. She was, however, sure that reading this book made her feel happy. Even more important, she was now aware of more choices and possible opportunities. Being made aware, opened up her mind. She liked the feeling of quiet excitement she received when reading it. Perhaps this book would take her on a new and exciting journey. She got another glass of iced tea and sat down to read some more.

# Five

# Setting Yourself Up For Success

*Love of Self—Step Towards Your Success*
Chapter 4 Do You Know What Makes You Happy?

Since you have the choice and the power to change your circumstances, it only makes sense to start making those choices right here and now. You are able to do this by choosing to focus on what you desire. The easiest way to make this choice is by choosing to love you first. Have respect for yourself, your thoughts, ideas, dreams, goals and desires. Respect and listen to what your heart and spirit say to your mind. When you remember to love yourself, you are then able to listen to your feelings, your heart, your desires and your spirits.

The information received includes the clues, directions, guidance and the next steps to take. Now, this may entail moving out of your comfort zone—out of an area that no longer serves you. That's right. Often that which once thought of or sought after for safety, is no longer the shelter that serves your new purpose. Of course you have the free will and choice to stay put, make one giant leap forward or to take many small steps ahead. The latter choices *remove* you from that which no longer serves you or is no longer in your best or new interest and will *propel* you towards that which is.

Coming from a space of love is easier than coming from a space of fear, as it is already closer to what you desire. However, ease is often not as relevant as the motivation or drive that starts the whole process of moving into action. Actions that are driven by something that *inspires* you as opposed to actions that have you feeling you *must* choose in order to be happy are far more productive and conducive to both your success and your truth.

Use this method as a guide for your first steps.

Step 1

Ask yourself, what kinds of things do you wish you were doing right now? With a pencil, pen, typewriter or computer, write out your wish list.

*"Life's like a movie; write your own ending, keep believing, keep pretending . . ." ~ Jim Henson*

Do you recall making a wish list for Santa when you were small? It would indeed be a great present you could gift yourself now by imagining that time of ease and innocence. While in that head space, write out your wish list. Nothing is out of the question. Nothing is too big or too small. Santa, after all, is capable of fulfilling all of your wishes. If Santa was not part of your upbringing then perhaps praying to, or conversing with some higher power may have been.

Again, like a child, imagine praying or asking for your heart's desires from a place of innocence, curiosity, wonder *and expectancy* that the wishes will be fulfilled. Place a smile on your face right now. If it helps to stick out your tongue while thinking, do that. Make ringlets in your hair with your finger; tap your chin; lie on your stomach on the floor or in the grass and think. Roll your eyes around to different locations so that you are able to access every type of dream, wish, circumstance, idea, or happenstance you desire to make manifest. Do it. Just do it. Let no thing or no one, including yourself, stop you from doing this simple act. Just simply, do it.

*"Choose again.*

*Pretend that you are enlightened.*
*Pretend that you are loved by God.*
*Pretend that you are perfect just the way you are.*

*Take a deep breath now and*
*PRETEND WHAT IS TRUE.*
*Then everything will make sense.*

*When you pretend something that is true, then you immediately*
*become that Truth.*

*First the energy of God descends upon the Earth, then it pretends*
*whatever it wants to be, then it ascends back to its source.*

*You are God pretending to be whatever you are right now.*
*Do you understand what this means?*

*You have allowed yourself to descend, but by pretending to be less*
*than what you are, you have not ascended back to God."*

*~ Thomas (Indigo Child)*

Step 2
   Now, note all of the objections that cross your mind (the "what-if" mind game).

   Write all of the negative self-speak, the dream busters, the nay sayings that Aunt Agatha would quip. Write them all down. This is your 'opponent's' "play book"—first hand information that you will *use to your own advantage*. With this collection of objections in hand, you have all of the possible oppositions that you may have to deal with up front and can go through them bit by bit, in your own time, and systematically *come up with realistic ways to overcome them*. How empowering is it to have up front knowledge about the possible events and to know that you are fully prepared and are able to triumph over them?

Do this assignment for each goal that you feel you'll need assistance in accomplishing. This single activity is so *very powerful* and so very successful in pinpointing possible protests and oppositions. Further, it gives you the arsenal necessary to ensure successful attainment of a goal, should you decide to take the steps necessary to take the goal to fruition.

Warning: when playing the "what-if" mind game, *be very careful not buy into the negatives yourself*. Don't let your dreams wither on the vine before the fruits have had a chance to mature! Yes, it is perfectly acceptable to choose not to pursue a goal; just be sure that you are making a conscious choice to discontinue for your own thought out reasons. Then, let it go. It's over and you have made a choice to make a new choice. Hurray!

It may be interesting to know that there are cases when a nay-sayer says what he says because of his *own* feelings of inadequacy. Past failures and past dealings in a similar situation when he was put down for having attempted a similar event, have coloured his response. Given the timing of the conversation, he may be going through a rough patch himself and is venting his frustrations onto you. In other words, it may be nothing to do with you and everything to do with only himself. *Try not to take things personally or literally*. Easier said than done, however, the rewards are worth the effort.

Step 3
　　Write out a typical day for you in the form of a schedule.

Write out the schedule so that it includes most everything from the time you normally get out of bed until the time that you normally climb back into bed. Include routines, predictable interruptions and anything else that comes to mind. Remember to include the weekend days as well. The following is a sample.

Day of the week: Mondays

| Time: | Activity |
|---|---|
| 5:30 a.m. | Hit snooze button |
| 6:00 a.m. | Groggily get out of bed |
| 6:10 a.m. | Look after own needs |
| 6:45 a.m. | Look after kids, dogs, cats etc. |
| ~~~~~~ | ~~~~~~~~~~~~~~~~~~~~~~~~ |
| 6:30 p.m. | Making supper, kids do their homework |
| ~~~~~~ | ~~~~~~~~~~~~~~~~~~~~~~~~ |
| 11:00 pm | Hit the hay |

# Step 4

The next step to take would be to see where you could choose to make some alterations to the schedule. Example:

Day of the week: Mondays

| Time: | Activity | Alternative A | Alternative B |
|---|---|---|---|
| 5:30 a.m. | Hit snooze button | Meditate | State affirmations |
| 6:00 a.m. | Groggily get up (frown and wish you could stay in bed instead) | Smile on purpose | Choose to have a magnificent day and make mental plans |
| 6:10 a.m. | Look after own needs (grumble about how cold it is in the room) | Look after own needs | Look after self—delegate some of the other responsibilities |
| 6:45 a.m. | Look after kids, dogs, cats etc. | Look after kids, dogs, cats etc. | Look after kids, etc. |
| ~~~~~~ | ~~~~~~~~~~~~~~~ | ~~~~~~~~~~~~~~~ | ~~~~~~~~~~~~~~~ |
| 6:00 p.m. | Make supper, kids do homework | Delegate supper, kids do their homework | Leftovers, facilitate homework |
| ~~~~~~ | ~~~~~~~~~~~~~~~ | ~~~~~~~~~~~~~~~ | ~~~~~~~~~~~~~~~ |
| 10:30 pm | Read in bed (push away dog/cat when they come for attention) | Write out / dictate into digital recorder the next days tasks | List tasks, choose clothes |
| 11:00 pm | Bed time—rehash what went right or wrong and restlessly fall asleep | Listen to recorded meditation and fall fast asleep zzz | Ask: What brings me joy? Record these thoughts and zzz |

Plan to take action. The cumulative effect of small changes in your life can pay off big time if you do them daily. Plan it out so that there is some dedicated time to carry out small, medium or large steps towards achieving the goals. **Always add in some fun activities, some down time, some family/friends/significant other time and some *you* time.**

Taking simple *inspired* actions (inspired actions: defined as following the intuition, listening to your heart and Spirit, acting on a strong impulse and hearing a calling) toward achievement of the goals will help attain it. The mere act of doing brings about a sense of accomplishment and raises your self-esteem. It leads to belief in you as a person of action and competence and is an act of honouring the self, demonstrating self love and thus leads to success.

Notice that inspired actions and working hard are mutually exclusive. Working hard often has its roots in fear of inaction leading to non-accomplishment of a goal or task. It can alternately lead to an unsatisfactory or disheartening accomplishment. Inspired action leads to doing things that feel right at the time, seem fun or inspirational, and seem logical. In other words, you would not feel resentful for having performed the task.

\*   \*   \*

Before this task is carried out, read the following. (Put down the pen or pencil. Move away from the typewriter. Shut off your computer screen.) Understand this—what ever people are currently doing *is* what they really want to do; it was their choice. Whether that choice was done consciously or subconsciously, it was still their choice to be where they are at this point in time.

In step one, the list that was created—the wish list—is just that, a wish list. The way to tell the difference between your wish and what you truly desire is to see what you *have*, are *doing* or how you are *behaving*. What you focus on expands and what you ignore contracts. So people *are* really doing what they really want to do in life. Whether the decision was performed consciously or unconsciously is immaterial.

The Law of Attraction, like the Law of Gravity, is constantly enforced. There is little choice in the matter here. By default, you are truly *doing* what you have chosen to do, are *having* the experiences that you have chosen to have and are *being* in the circumstances that you have chosen to be. You make your living as you do because you often chose to not use your creative power to create the life that you deserve. You have the power to create a life that you deserve? Yes! Furthermore, you deserve a life of happiness and magnificence; all of us do! It is another thing that you were born with.

*The power of free will, choice and deserving whatever you focus and act upon,* are the gifts given to you as your birthright. Does this statement resonate within you as truth at this time? If it does, great! If it doesn't, that fine too! It's okay if this truth does not currently register as truth because in time, it will. (How wonderful it is to have finally been exposed to the truth!)

Free will and choice give you the right to agree, the right to agree to disagree and the right to just plain disagree. It's all okay. Eventually, you all see the truth for what it is and then you shift and move into higher levels of consciousness; all in Good time; Divine time. You each have a choice to make the life that you want from where you are right now. You each have the power to bring to yourself all that you require in order to fulfill your dreams; people, money, circumstances and resources. It stems and starts from the inside, not the outside.

\*     \*     \*

Kelly wondered what made her happy. She had never thought of *having* choices to make her world the way she would want it to be. What a concept! All this time she had just been living her life, one day at a time, reacting to the circumstances that happened to her. She lived in reaction—at the *effect* of what occurred. Not once had she ever considered that she was not always at the *cause* of her own life. Nor had it occurred to her that she was the designer or the creator of her own life.

Kelly remembered how excited she would get when she wrote her letter to Santa. The games . . . the toys . . . the craft supplies . . . records, ribbons, books and more. She felt giddy once more as she planned her list for "Santa" to fill. Hmm, she thought. No ribbons, toys or records listed this time. Well, no little kid toys, anyway. A new car would be nice. Her old car Daisy was truly on her last wheels.

She laughed after she had listed the objections. They were easier to come up with than the desires. Darn, she thought. Why are negatives so easy to find?

For step three, Kelly chose to look at her Friday schedule. She felt lost on Fridays. Tim's life was taken on a Friday. Now it was time to reclaim them.

Charlie came up to her, purring and rubbing up against her leg. Bedtime. "Are you ready for bed there, Chuck?" More purring met her query. Suddenly Kelly felt very sleepy and decided to call it a night. "Come on, Handsome, let's go to bed." She placed the guidebook, papers and pen on the coffee table and stood up. Charlie ran ahead of her, tail held high. As he entered the room, he suddenly stopped to groom his back. As she walked towards the bedroom, thoughts of what she had read and wrote filled her head and held her attention. Preoccupied with this, Kelly didn't see the cat in the doorway and nearly tripped over him, bringing her back into the present moment. Charlie jumped up onto the chair and then took his place on the bed.

Kelly dressed for bed, combed her hair and then climbed under the covers. As she settled for slumber, the words of the little book came back to her mind. Making a wish list and a vision schedule was an easy and low risk way to step out of her self-imposed box to think new thoughts and possibilities. She was inspired toward including some new and fun experiences. As she drifted off, a smile formed on her lips. How wonderful Fridays were going to be once more, she thought. She was certainly looking forward to doing step four tomorrow. Soon afterward, Kelly was fast asleep.

\*     \*     \*

In her dream state, Kelly saw herself doing what she considered to be wonderful and fantastical things. She met a man who looked a lot like Tim. He shared some tips on creative wish making. The man encouraged her to "wish from the end" where, instead of wishing to be a ballerina, seeing the experience from an *observers point of view*, wish from the point of seeing herself as the ballerina in the current time, *through her own eyes*. Feel the muscles ache after practice, see the audience smiling at her performance, hear the roar of the applause and encores as the curtain comes down. In other words, be in the head space as if you are living your wish, already having your wish and happily using and enjoying your wish.

"*You create from within*", the man in her dream said. You start at the heart space where all inspired actions are possible and probable. You show love to yourself by honouring your wishes and dreams and taking steps toward having those wishes and dreams fulfilled. Fulfilled dreams and wishes benefit the creator and the world at large; a win-win situation.

The man's grin at his win-win statement was what Kelly remembered the most upon *awakening*. Her furry alarm clock must have been out hunting his catnip mouse prey, as he was not in her bedroom. It was a treat to have time to think before getting out of bed on a cool Saturday morning. She lay in bed an extra half hour mulling over the thoughts inspired by all this new information. The sun shone through the slats in the blinds.

Blue sky could be seen by peeking out the window. Kelly rose, donned a robe and headed for the kitchen. She started the water for coffee and prepared the drip filter in the cone. Soon wafts of a delicious aroma came to her nostrils. She filled her favourite glass coffee cup and headed towards the front door.

The morning paper stared up at her and Kelly picked it up. Coffee and paper in hand, she sat down on the couch ready to do her daily routine of thumbing through the headlines, reading the horoscope page, checking her biorhythms and doing the Sudoku and crossword puzzles. The Comics page was fished out and set aside to be read later on in the bathroom. As the page landed on the coffee table, Kelly saw the pen, paper and the little manual that she had acquired the day before. While thumbing through the newspaper, she found her mind was still distracted by the material she had read and the task that she was inspired to do last night. Reading about the doom and gloom that took place in her world did not fit in with accomplishing her wishes and dreams.

Kelly chuckled at the thought of herself accomplishing fantastical things. Before yesterday, she would have been reading her paper and thinking how terrible her world was. Before yesterday, such optimistic thoughts would never have crossed her mind. Before yesterday, those possibilities did not exist. A lot has happened since yesterday, she thought.

She put down the newspaper and picked up the little book once more. After re-reading Part 4, she happily set to the task of making her Fridays a little brighter. All of the ideas that she had before drifting off to sleep came rushing back. She plugged them in their respective slots; tongue sticking out to one side like it did when she was a little girl. Happy with her accomplishment, she put down the pen and read over her new Friday schedule. Not bad at all Kel, she thought. Not bad at all. With that being said and done, she set off toward the kitchen for a refill on her coffee.

# Six

# Are You Content With Mediocrity?

*Love of Self—Step Towards Your Success*
Chapter 5 There Is a Powerful Force Within You

You begin the creation process from within. If you do not go within, you go without. You go without if you do not first go within. People don't always do what they dislike doing, or even feel that they *have* to do. They make their decisions with the information at hand and choose their best option. With the presentation of *this* information, there is now a new option to consider. By following new thoughts, ideas, attitudes, words, beliefs, choices and expectations your current circumstances will start to change. Are you content with mediocrity? To continue choosing the same old options gets the same old results. Only by choosing new options can different results be had. It's that simple.

When you move in the direction of doing things that make you happy, it brings you joy, motivates you and inspires you into action. It also gets your creative juices flowing, and is an act of self love. You must still continue to do your duties and fulfill your responsibilities. Ignoring them too often or for too long brings other hardships. Ignoring them creates imbalance in another direction.

Taking new steps towards your dreams will create wonderful results for you and for others. You'll feel happy; others will notice and feel happy. The ripple effect will come into play, touching more people than you could ever imagine. Fulfill obligations and go in the direction of your dreams. Make arrangements to delegate some of your responsibilities to free up a little more private time. You have people and/or beings on your side who wish to support you in your endeavours. Use them.

Self love allows and gives you permission to do the things that bring you joy and success in many ways into your lives. Real successful people listen to their hearts regardless of what others say. They take chances to express their desires outside of themselves. Successful people do not keep their hopes, dreams and desires inside. The dreams do not die within them or with them—they get expressed! Acts of self love are your keys and tickets to success.

*"... Our deepest fear is not that we are inadequate. Our deepest fear is that we are powerful beyond measure. It is our light, not our darkness, that most frightens us . . . . Your playing small doesn't serve the world. There's nothing enlightened about shrinking so that other people won't feel insecure around you. We are all meant to shine . . . to make manifest the glory of God . . . within us . . . everyone. And as we let our own light shine, we unconsciously give other people permission to do the same. As we're liberated from our own fear, our presence . . . liberates others . . ." ~ From* A RETURN TO LOVE *by Marianne Williamson*

Sometimes, when you look at some of the things that you want to express, the risks and the tasks seem too big and overwhelming. However, if you are truthful with yourself and truly look at the parts and break them down into small chunks, then you can see that it is your fear of the large picture that scares you into immobility. You have turned this fear into some new behaviours and false beliefs. These behaviours and beliefs have turned into self-imposed restrictions and excuses that you use to keep yourself limited and in check.

Little tasks such as calling a friend, looking at a fabric swatch, deciding which colour would look better, which item tastes the best and so on, are not too difficult to make. You are very capable of choosing to release, getting over and allowing yourself to be freed from your own self-imposed prisons. But . . . first you must realize and admit to yourself that you *are* imprisoned and that you have been placed there by your own self, consciously or subconsciously.

Finally, you need to get the courage to love yourself enough to leave the shelter of this often self-imposed prison by doing something about it. Of course you always have the option of staying where you are, doing and experiencing what is familiar. And furthermore, you can gripe and grumble about it to anyone and everyone who will grant you an audience—including yourself! However, the better choice is to pick yourself up, dust yourself off and go off in a new direction. It can be just one baby-step after another. Progress is progress.

The powerful old saying of *"a journey of a thousand miles begins with a single step"* (attributed to Lao Tzu—*founder of Taoism*) certainly applies here. **If you don't ever start, it will never happen at all!**

Ultimately**,** *"It's not the mountain we conquer but ourselves."* *~ Sir Edmund Hillary*. By conquering fear and caring about yourself—thus demonstrating *you* care about *you*—that *you* are important and do matter—is truly a wonderful and loving thing to do for all of us, *to* all of us.

*       *       *

The more she read, the more she wanted to read. This little book had some great ideas, she thought. Kelly began to feel a stirring from within; an excitement that comes with new and renewed hope and inspiration. She began to think back to when she was a little girl. How odd her dream had seemed to her and especially to her friends and a lot of her family.

"What do you want to be when you grow up, Kelly?" asked her aunt.

"A philanthropist!" she answered.

Kelly had read about the great things that great people were doing for others in her books. People helping people. Usually it was the rich helping out the poor, but not all philanthropists were rich in money. Some were rich in spirit, kindness, assistance, guidance and inspiration. The common thread was that all were givers. They gave what they could to those in need. Those who were helped were grateful for the gifts they received and often went on to help others in turn.

Aunt Emily made an attempt at a smile and commented that only wealthy people could afford such luxury. Her aunt further pointed out that she did not have any resources to draw upon to fulfil that dream. It would be best to choose a sensible occupation to pursue.

Kelly saw the look on her parents' faces. They did not know what to say. Kelly then surmised that a philanthropist was not an appropriate choice for her and started considering other alternatives.

That year, a lot of unfortunate events occurred and Kelly had to mature quickly, beyond her years. Coming out of that thought, Kelly wiped her eyes and got up for some more coffee. She returned with some rye toast and a fresh cup of coffee, then began to read some more.

# Seven

## Do a *Local* Motion

*Love of Self—Step Towards Your Success*
  Chapter 6 There Is Another Powerful Force Within You

By listening to their hearts people have another way to listen to what the Creator is encouraging everyone to do. With your spirit being part of the Great Spirit, you have a direct line to God. You are a part of Him, still connected to Him. If you make the choice to listen to your heart, you will find yourself being guided along the journey that you focus upon. You truly are *never* alone.

*"The best and most beautiful things in the world cannot be seen nor touched . . . but are felt in the heart"*—Helen Keller

People will rarely be spontaneously guided to pursue a path that they themselves have not already started to travel. In other words, Spirit will not tell you to go left or right if you are not already heading in that particular direction. But, when you ask for directions or guidance as to the road that would be in your highest and best interest to take, that is another story. You will always be given an answer when you ask for guidance and direction.

*"Two roads diverged in a yellow wood, and sorry I could not travel both, and be one traveler, long I stood and looked down one as far as I could . . . Two roads diverged in a wood, and I—I took the one less traveled by, and that has made all the difference."* Frost's words speak the truth.

You are all travelers in this world. Every day you are presented with choices to make. Sometimes there are more than two roads that lie in front of us. Some are safe, some are unknown. When given the choice, many people choose to go on the path that everyone else has taken . . . just to be safe. Safe is a lie that you often choose to tell yourself is real. Nothing in this world is safe. There is no sure thing. There are no guarantees. Playing it safe or doing what everyone else has always done will only lead to one destination—the place where everyone else who played it safe ended up: nowhere you have not been before; the same old same old. If you want to be phenomenally successful and lead a life filled with joy and abundance, then you have to diverge from the beaten path and take the road less traveled.

Listen. Hear the answer from within, from a friend, from a song, from a book. The answer will always show up when you need it. You don't even have to wait until you "need" it the "most" either. Many people refuse to hear until, out of sheer desperation, they are willing to "give it a try" and go within (as they've gone without long enough in their minds). You can even ask if the path that you chose is the right one at this point in time and be given an answer. Having free will and choice also means that you must first use your will, make your choice and then correct and continue.

Inertia is the resistance of any physical object to a change in its state of motion. Sir *Isaac Newton's* first Law of Motion is often stated as: An object at rest tends to stay at rest and an object in motion tends to stay in motion with the same speed and in the same direction *unless acted upon by an unbalanced* *force*. Inertia comes from the Latin word, "iners", meaning idle, or lazy.*[1] Hmm; another law. Isn't it funny how these natural laws just keep cropping up? Yet, you'd be wise to take heed of them, as they are part of the human experience here on Earth.

*Get involved in your own life!* Use your voice. Be part of the process and speak up! In this instance and in this process, you should never compromise either yourself or your Creator. In this process, you are putting yourself back in touch with both yourself and Spirit and with life itself. You stop dying and start living—truly living—not merely going through the motions of living.

So, "dance like no one's watching". Say no to the nay sayers and say yes to you!

\*     \*     \*

Kelly had come across some questionable inspirational books before. They seemed to have "sure fire" ways and methods that promised the moon and the stars. She had also come across some really solid books that gave sound advice. Some of the sound advice actually did help, Kelly thought. But life went on and she was not always seeking to make changes in her life. Now, however, it seemed a little different. This book spoke to her at the heart level. It brought back the dreams of a little girl who was carefree and wanting more out of life. It reignited that spark that she once had. Before yesterday, such optimistic thoughts would never have crossed her mind.

After a last bite of her toast, Kelly placed her little plate on the floor near the cat's dish. It had a few dregs of butter on it. Charlie loved getting this special treat. Kelly returned to the living room, curled up on the couch and resumed her reading.

# Eight

## Believe in Yourself

*Love of Self—Step Towards Your Success*
Chapter 7 What's Luck Got to Do with It? or The Games People Play!

*"Oh the games people play now, every night and every day now, never meaning what they say now, never saying what they mean . . ."*
~ *Merle Haggard*

This chapter deals with dreams and outcomes. Read the information and allow the lesson to sink in.

For the record, there are a number of people who chose to get up the courage to believe differently than they have in the past. They felt empowered! They felt alive! They walked tall with their head held high. They looked every bit the champion. That is until what they believed in, put their hopes upon, poured their hearts and souls into and felt was a sure thing, did not come about as expected. They did everything that they could think of: thought right, took the right steps, played by the rules, prayed, convinced their friends, family and acquaintances that it was going to happen for sure, ignored the nay sayers, stuck to their guns, were steadfast in their convictions and did everything else they felt was necessary for the guarantee of the outcome. They did all of the above—played the game—and lost. Then they were devastated and either became angry, bitter or really sad. "What a waste of time!" "How could I have been so stupid?" "Where was God when I needed him?" "It's not fair!" So, what's the point in following your dreams? Read on.

What these people failed to remember was their original intent or idea. They had decided to play a *game*. Games are fun! Their purposes are to either entertain or challenge you. With their varied rules, regulations, structures and themes, games come in a vast variety of forms. Furthermore, people make up new ones to play all of the time! And why not? They're enjoyable to play and entertaining to watch. Games are a chance to be involved in an activity and have a little fun. You take pleasure in the time, or ride, while it lasts, and then everyone goes home. A few have something in their hands when they leave. But many, in fact most, simply leave with a memory as their prize and memento.

Games of chance, such as winning the lottery, a new car, a cruise, a dream vacation or that lovely dream home are just that—a game. Games usually have only one main winner. They are meant to bring hope to the participants. Hope brings on good feelings. Good feelings bring on endorphins (a natural chemical reaction in the body). Endorphins make people feel happy. Happy people focus on and attract more good things their way than unhappy people. In fact, your life here on Earth is just one big game that you've all agreed to play; complete with structure, rules, regulations, winners, losers, start and stop time. The contestants agree to play roles where they are the opposite of what they truly are. In reality, the contestants are truly beings of infinite power simply wanting to experience something other than boredom and their own greatness. They are part of a greater whole, seeking knowledge and understanding of what it would feel like if; they lived in lack, fear and hopelessness; had a disability; were at a disadvantage; created pain, joy or sorrow; felt pain, joy or sorrow; the list is endless.

*"And they while away the hours, in their ivory towers, till they're covered up with flowers in the back of a black limousine." ~ Merle Haggard*

But a game is a game is a game. A Mathematical Law states: a constant is a constant is a constant. (Yep, another law.) You pay your money and take your chances. It's a little thrill. The key concept that some people fail to realize is: *You are paying your money living on Earth, simply for the thrill/hope, for the ride/experience, or for the cause/something bigger than yourself.*

An example of causes that are bigger than yourself would be the Big Brothers and Big Sisters societies; helping hospitals, research money for the cure of ailments, helping the children, feeding the poor, making a dying person's dream come true and so on. Your ticket money is used to help fund these worthy projects and the prizes that you *may* win. Your contribution is used and, like in the lottery, gives you a *chance* at winning a prize—not a *guarantee* at winning a prize. Do *not* hang all of your dreams on a star that you are not *guaranteed* to be able to lasso. Why would you? Why set yourself up for failure or disappointment? Because you MIGHT win? Well, yes and no.

The thrill of victory is a fantastic feeling. And of course, there are few guarantees in life so go ahead and play games. Winning is a wonderful experience. It brings about more feelings of high intensity. It feels great for the hour, day, week, month or year. But make no mistake. That high will never be sustained for ever. Even with the powerful memory that you have, or the trophy that you can gaze upon, or the intermittent "atta boy" that is received, a prize will only sustain you for as long as you can hold onto that feeling or memory. (And you know that it is not all that long of a time, especially in the grand scheme of things.) Know this. Understand the intention behind playing games and you will hardly ever allow a "loss" to ruin your life and dreams.

This is not to say never participate in a game, in the lottery or the draw ever again—no! This is to clarify the reason behind games—any game—is to have fun, feel uplifted, be inspired, take action, get high on life, smile a little broader, be child-like and feel the wonder, joy and possibilities of what might be. For without games, there is precious little else that is able to happily distract you from your everyday life.

*"You will become as small as your controlling desire, or as great as your dominant aspiration"* - Mark Victor Hansen.

By the way, this includes "get rich quick" games and schemes. Sometimes people need to feel or think that they are able to lasso a star. It's a process that teaches many great lessons. Choose the lessons with care, my friend. If there is a win—great! If there is not a win—great! There is an opportunity for growth and maturity that is *far more valuable than the money*, time or labour lost.

Games give you the opportunity to join with others in great (and not so great) endeavours. Whether that endeavour involves being a grand World Champion at Tidily Winks or Monopoly or having bragging rights that the Oranges are better at basketball than their arch rivals, the Apples; games give you the chance to test your mettle.

If your cause is to help raise funds for a new library or just to prove that you are greater than the sea by swimming the English Channel; these games indicate to you who you are and what you stand for. They teach you to behave in a manner that illustrates "good sportsmanship", win or lose.

Playing a game is a chance or opportunity to *freely* participate and *choose* the avenue that you desire. You can *focus* you attention on an outcome that you'd like to see. Sometimes you win, sometimes you don't, but it is definitely not the final outcome that is the prize. You would be wise to learn not to be too attached to that. It is the process and the experience and the learning about *yourself* that is your reward. Indeed, that is the ultimate, real and true prize.

Know this as well: No *one* and no *thing*, including people, Spirit, fate or Satan, is out to "get us". (Neale Donald Walsch, in his "Conversations with God" series, says that there is no such thing as Satan. SATAN is an acronym for *Seeing All Things As Negative.*) If anything, you are the one who sets yourself up for a fall (especially when you fail to ask yourself, "Is this in my highest and best interest?").

Entertaining the thought that someone or something is out to get you is an defeatist way to think. An uninformed person has few life experiences to base important decisions upon or is a person without full knowledge of polarities to choose between the negatives and positives.

Sometimes it *is* in your *best interest* to play the game, be involved, take that chance—*not* because you are *guaranteed* to win, but *because of the golden opportunities that you come across along the way.* You might meet people you might never have met before, had thoughts that you would not have had or entertained in the past, felt feelings of joy, hope, desire, excitement and fun. You might do things that you haven't done in a while or felt interested in doing for a long time, like holding hands. Perhaps holding that kiss a little longer, playing with the dog. You might be taking better care of yourself and your loved ones. All in all, feeling like a kid in a candy store with lots of money in his pocket to spend!

It is possible you'll hear opinions that are different and therefore stretch your views a little more or have the opportunity to be involved in something greater than yourself. Maybe you'll have taken time out from your everyday life and remembered what having fun is all about again. When you remember to have fun and are inspired, you re-member with the collective and make the world a better place to be.

Well, here you are again; another chance for choosing to be self-loving and having success in your life.

*　*　*

Kelly found this chapter to be a bit confusing. Why would a book advocating and encouraging love of self (being successful in your endeavours and taking risks to follow your dreams, quite simply, in effect, changing your life) put your worst fears right there in black and white?

She re-read parts to get more of a firm grasp of this last chapter. It helped to laser her focus on the message and its meaning. Games are for fun, entertainment, learning opportunities, testing one's mettle and for bragging rights. There are highs and lows and learning how to gracefully handle both sides while participating in games. Kelly figured that sports, including the Olympics, would qualify in that area. Rides, board games, card games and even kids games would also fall into that category as well. Games of chance and gambling seemed to be in a slot all of their own.

Kelly recalled a time when she had purchased a ticket on a dream home. She had truly felt that she would win the top prize. She visited the home, took pictures of herself in the home, she had even wrote out the address re-direct cards to be posted in the mail for when she won. She did everything listed in those Law of Attraction books, including the *"set it and forget it" (Ron Popeil)* part. Kelly remembered just how devastated she felt when she found out that she was *not* the grand prize winner, nor a winner of *anything* from that lottery. It took her almost three weeks to get over that shock to her system.

Now Kelly finally understood why doing all the right things did not work nor matter much either. She was in the wrong place. It wasn't that God didn't want her to have that new home; it was that she was playing a game and forgot that she was playing a game. Oh, she had fun feeling happy and feeling great about the possibility of winning. Nevertheless, it was a game that could be either won or lost. The outcome was not the important thing; it was the journey along the way. She recalled how confident she felt during those weeks before the draw. Things just seemed to go her way—big things, little things, things that mattered and things that didn't really matter all that much. In fact she was on such a high that she figured she was assured to win that dream home.

Looking back, Kelly felt how lucky she was to have had such a wonderful streak of luck. Nothing special had really happened at that point; she had simply purchased a ticket. Yet she felt happy during those weeks; really happy. She had dreamed a little bigger, walked a little taller and thought happy positive thoughts. In fact, Kelly could not recall a single time that she had let anything bother her. There were no self put-downs, no giving in to negative comments, few feelings of fear and no dreading real or imagined situations. Kelly was indeed a fortunate soul to have had such a *"winning streak"*. She was glad to have finally learned the Truth.

*　　*　　*

Kelly recalled a little more of her dream. It had to do with dreaming and getting excited about possible changes in her life. In the dream, she heard herself say, "The more I allow myself to let go of fear, the more I can control the changes. I choose to be in control of those changes. I can choose to make positive changes and be okay with those changes. I can choose to be in charge of my changing. In following my dreams, I will attain skills, knowledge, information and self-confidence that will pave the way for success in future endeavours." Kelly remembered feeling happy, confident and inspired in her dream. People were coming up to her, thanking her for taking the chance to share her gift with the world. She wished she knew what gift she had shared that had caused such heartfelt appreciation from her "fans".

The phone rang. Kelly put down her book and answered the phone. It was her sister-in-law, Marla.

"Hi Kel," the warm voice on the other end of the phone said. "How 'ya doin'?" Kelly and Marla exchanged pleasantries and chatted about the weather and what not. Hoping that Marla could shed some light on her dream, Kelly brought up last night's vision.

Marla listened intently. It was rare for Kelly to chat about anything for an extended period of time, let alone ask for assistance in her life. Marla thought carefully before she said anything. She felt that this was very important to Kelly in some big way. Marla observed that the dream was telling Kelly that she was ready for change. The Buddhist proverb, *When the student is ready the teacher will appear*, came to mind. Marla shared that perhaps Kelly was going to come across, if she had not already, some valuable information. She advised Kelly to be open to benefit from the awareness, data and information given by people who have explored, learned well and embraced reflection. "Look for people who have investigated their potential and are willing to share their insights with you, Kel," said Marla.

Marla shared an episode from her own life that had taken place in her early university years. She had learned to pay attention and take heed of people who appear at the right time with their guidance and information. Their support was of great benefit to her journey and the direction that it had taken.

A professor of hers had shared some of his insights in a discussion they had on Marla's possible future in teaching or some other field. The professor had shared his observations of her gifts. He had commented to Marla about how impressed he was with the way that she had talked to the other students in her class. Furthermore, he had observed how they had left with understanding and joy in their step after reflecting upon her information and suggestions.

Marla shared that she had not seen herself or her style of interacting in quite the way that he had stated. The professor had felt that although Marla had great potential in several directions, that pursuit in the field of education would be an excellent direction for her to take. Marla stated, "Now, I'm glad that I pursued teaching special needs children over different paths that I had felt were easier and far less risky to take on. It's what gave me confidence in myself and moulded me into the person that I am today."

One comment made by Marla had made a particular impression on Kelly. Marla had said, "Whenever I felt discouraged, I remembered that moment and kept on keeping on in my endeavours. It gave me something to lean on and the strength to move forward." Kelly liked the picture she got as she envisioned Marla overcoming and triumphing over her obstacles.

Kelly and Marla chatted a little more. "Hey, I'd like to read that book that Steve said you were reading. It sounds interesting." Marla said. Kelly agreed to let her have it as soon as she was finished. They said their good-byes and Kelly hung up the phone.

Thinking a break from reading so intently would do her some good, Kelly went into the kitchen to get a glass of water. Charlie came up to her, purring as usual. As she absentmindedly stroked the large white cat's fur, her mind wandered to her telephone conversation with Marla. Should she strive to better herself through new beliefs? What types of changes would she be undergoing that could ever lead to having fans? And what of this latest chapter on games of chance? How did this all fit in?

"*. . . golden opportunities that you come across along the way.*" Is the book suggesting that choosing to be self-loving is a golden opportunity? A chance to show if not to anyone else but our own self, "*. . . who you are and what you stand for*" It would seem that it all starts with me; within me. I need to choose to have, do or be the experience that I want to have happen; to make manifest, as Marla would say. I need to consciously direct what I want to experience. Is this what the book is saying? Curiosity got the better of Kelly and she decided to read further on to find out more information.

# Nine

## Have a Nice *Trip*!

*Love of Self—Step Towards Your Success*
Chapter 8 Do We Set Ourselves up for a Fall?

Sometimes when people are inspired and set out to accomplish a great task—especially one that requires a lot of personal time, energy, money and commitment, they inadvertently set themselves up to fail. Often referred to as a victim mentality, this process can very quickly and easily place people in a downward spiral. This results in situations that are worse than they were before. To the *victims*, it appears as if something inevitably happens, often at the worst possible time. They believe that they are at the effect of someone or something. Rarely, if ever, do they see themselves at the cause of their plight. Victim mentality can show itself in a several different forms.

First, in the form of *self-doubt* and *fear of success*; people think that they are following their dreams and taking the right steps, but the pieces do not seem to fall into place. Inadvertently on a subconscious level, they have left out steps that they knew were necessary to the success of the project. Perhaps they chose to ignore some sage piece of advice and then are bewildered as to why their dreams are not coming true. They have *self-sabotaged* the process almost from the very beginning.

Second, in the form of *denial*; this group of people want to do it all by themselves and refuse to accept offers of assistance from others. Their pride prevents them from allowing the love of others to offer support, aid or facilitate their dreams into manifestation. In doing so, this group miss out on opportunities, critical information, timing and a host of other things. They end up blaming the whole world for their shortcomings.

Third, in entertaining a belief that there are people or *forces* that are out there to "get them," some people have inexplicable things occur. They blame their "enemies" or God, or some unseen form of darkness or dark forces; the list can be quite long. It was their own negative belief that caused the occurrence of mishaps.

Finally, there are some people who value themselves as being so *insignificant* that they allow others such as family, friends and strangers to bully, manipulate and take advantage of them. The only form of "control" that this group has is to either elicit the sympathy of others by plying their true story tales of woe, or crying and carrying on to force others to look after them, make decisions for them and cater to them.

It serves nobody to be bullied, controlled, or coerced, nor does it serve anyone to bully, control or coerce. There is no form of love present there. (Of course, when anyone is in danger, you need to give aid. *Then, you must respect what choices they make* after being helped out of difficult situations as you all have the right to free will and choice.)

*"People take different roads seeking fulfillment and happiness. Just because they're not on your road doesn't mean they've gotten lost."* ~ H. Jackson Brown, Jr.

Remember that to turn the other cheek does not mean to do so in order for it to be slapped too, but rather, to turn the head around and go off into a new direction, make a new choice and walk away from your current situation. It matters not whether the slap comes from bullies, friends, family or strangers. Nor does it matter if the slap comes from our self (in the form of negative thought patterns, beliefs or behaviours). It doesn't serve a worthwhile purpose to stay stuck. Let go (not from a place of fear or judgement) from a place of love.

At the other extreme, you have a *bully mentality*. This group set themselves up to win—to succeed—no matter the cost. Bully mentality can show itself in a few different forms as well. One form portrays itself with a layer of over-confidence over an interior of fear. This form is recognizable by them being quick to anger, yell or some other appearance of being out of control when faced with non-compliance or defeat.

Another form is in the use of *snide remarks* and *put-downs* (which can also be masked as back-handed compliments.) This lot uses a passive-aggressive approach to control others. They belittle others to feel superior. Sometimes this tactic is stumbled upon when they get what they want from sensitive people who would usually give in at the sound of a loud voice or cutting remark. Often this group was controlled with negative words or threats themselves. They are often unaware that theirs is a learned behaviour which they disliked when it was directed at them. All too often they mimic and mirror what they have grown up with in their own lives. They also have not made a conscious choice to change this pattern at this time.

There is also a group who simply *act before they think*. Words like, "I'm only doing this because I love you," "Okay honey, but it really did look like a disaster," or "I just don't feel like going," can be heard. This group will appear to agree then spew out a cutting remark or will compromise, but make a big production of it. Sometimes favours, affection or support are withheld.

Regardless of the form, manipulation is manipulation. Even when they "give in", they still have others feeling intimidated. It will often be a very long time before these others are willing to undertake another round. So, in fact, although the bullies may have lost that one fight, they still ended up winning the war and often they know it, too.

Finally, there is a group who, not unlike the victim mentality crowd, value themselves as being so *insignificant* that they turn on themselves, manipulate and loathe themselves so much that they take it out on others. The only form of "control" that this group has is to either explode or implode. They hurt others or they hurt themselves.

The bottom line is that on some level, these groups of behaviours are often rooted in fear and insecurity. They dread the thought of not being in control. Does this make them "bad or weak" people? No. (Lost and misguided, they are in need of self-love and support from others. This group will be able to do what they need to do to be both successful and feel happy and safe inside . . . if.)

With this information in hand, if you find that things are not going as planned, check to make sure that a victim or bully mentality is not part of the equation. If it is, a reset of your thinking and beliefs is necessary, before true success can be attained. Life seems to be quirky that way. Once made aware and after some initiative has been taken, the most important task is . . . love of self. Life allows for other opportunities to appear and come into fruition. Life on Earth seems to have some basic rules that need to be followed if you are to truly have a happy and successful life.

*     *     *

Kelly put down the manuscript, lay down on the couch and closed her eyes. As she was digesting this chapter's message, thoughts of her brother Steve came to mind. Steve would serve as an excellent role model for how to successfully accomplish whatever a person's heart wished. He did it with grace, ease, integrity, tenacity, the right attitude and had fun or at the very least enjoyed the process, regardless of its outcome. How does he do it? Kelly was no wall flower or a bully, yet she didn't have the same quality of life that Steve had. When did she loose that spark and childlike curiosity of life?

"Do I set myself up for a fall?" Kelly wondered. She thought about her internal dialog and the choices she habitually made. "Do I create pain in my life," she pondered. "Are there subtle ways that I have mastered that make me a victim?" Kelly recognized that fear and self-doubt were often a part of her way of life.

Kelly decided that she was no longer going to continue victimizing herself. She was going to change that. Kelly chose love over fear and felt happier because of her self-loving choice. She resolved to fix the problem by emulating optimistic, balanced and proactive people. Steve, Marla and Monika came to mind.

The year 2010 not only started a new year, but a new decade as well. She thought about her friend Monika and her Facebook post for the New Year.

*'Monika wonders if starting off the New Year with a full moon that's blue will make 2010 a stellar year? I'm betting YES!*

*Happy New Year to one and all! May you all achieve the goals that you set, be granted the wishes you hope to come true and have a few too many pleasant surprises happen along the way.*

*Love, light, life and laughter to one and all!'*

Her upbeat friend had not had a stellar year for a long time, yet ever the optimist, she always had a smile upon her face. Kelly wished her friend many super stellar years to come, starting with this one, starting right now.

Kelly wrote a note for herself to call her friend tomorrow. A coffee date would allow the two a chance to reconnect and a chance for Kelly to bounce around a few ideas with her friend. She placed down the pen and picked up her book once more.

# Ten

# Fantasized Experiences *Appearing* Realistic

*Love of Self—Step Towards Your Success*
Chapter 9 A Note About Fears

Fear can be a strong motivator to get yourself out of dire, difficult or uncomfortable situations. It can also act as a key factor that puts your life on hold or limits your full capacity in one way or another.

Fear can take on a variety of forms.

- Fear of success
- Fear of failure
- Fear of rejection
- Fear of being abandoned/alone
- Fear of emotional pain
- Fear of being judged
- Fear of embarrassment
- Fear of expressing true feelings
- Fear of responsibility
- Fear of change
- Fear of intimacy
- Fear of commitment
- Fear of the unknown
- Fear of loss
- Fear of death

When you experience success, failure, rejection, abandonment or emotional pain, you tend to react to them. Being judged or embarrassed provides different feelings to deal with. When expressing your true feelings, facing change, responsibility, times of intimacy, the unknown, loss or death, you deal with other emotions.

How you choose to deal with any situation, is up to you. Obviously, the more self confident you are in yourself and the more you feel you are loved, including loving your own self, generally the more easily you handle any situation. Furthermore, all of these fears can be met and overcome if you are open and willing to take the time and *appropriate sized* steps to conquer them; in effect, turning mountains into mole-hills.

*"In addition to the . . . basic fears, there is another **evil**\* by which people suffer . . . . let us call this **evil** SUSCEPTIBILITY TO NEGATIVE INFLUENCES . . . . Recognize that you . . . are, by nature . . . susceptible to all suggestions which harmonize with your weaknesses . . . . set up habits for the purpose of counteracting all these fears. Recognize that negative influences often work through your subconscious mind . . . Your mind is your spiritual estate! Protect and use it with the care to which Divine Royalty is entitled."*
~ *Napoleon Hill, Think and Grow Rich*

* *"God did not create evil. **Evil** is in the absence of God in people's hearts; it is in the absence of love, humanity and faith. Love and faith are like heat and light. They exist. Their absence leads to evil."* ~ *Albert Einstein*

* *"**Evil** (ignorance) is like a shadow—it has no real substance of its own, it is simply a lack of light. You cannot cause a shadow to disappear by trying to fight it, stamp on it, by railing against it, or any other form of emotional or physical resistance. In order to cause a shadow to disappear, you must shine light on it."* ~ *Shakti Gawain*

Without really realizing it, you often give in to fear and give up your power in subtle ways. For example: putting your basic needs last, suffering in silence, offering compliance, saying yes when you want to or should say no, having few or weak boundaries, putting up with situations and allowing others to influence you in ways that affect your thoughts and feelings in uncomfortable and negative ways.

What are some ways or activities that give power to you and help you feel empowered? Formulating original ideas, setting up clear boundaries, standing up for yourself and saying no, making a decision and sticking to it and achieving a goal (start small—it really is for the better—it builds a firm foundation for larger and larger goals) and finally, creating something.

*"Your vision will become clear only when you can look into your own heart. Who looks outside, dreams, who looks inside awakens."*
*~ Carl Jung*

Consider gaining self-awareness by asking yourself: what makes you happy, what brings you joy, what bugs you, would it be better if you took this path or that path? Instead of fearing change, make a deliberate conscious choice to actually cherish change. Think of change as an opportunity for growth and maturity. Constantly remind yourself, if you start to panic and get upset, to graciously accept change and all the wonderful results that come with it.

Further, consider being receptive to the responses of your questions. By becoming more aware of your thoughts, feelings and desires, you are attracting the circumstances sought after in your life.

*"The road to happiness lies in two simple principles: find what interests you and that you can do well, and put your whole soul into it—every bit of energy and ambition and natural ability you have."—John D. Rockefeller*

Meditation is a type of inner listening and a way of being receptive. A stronger awareness and connection with God, with the One, and with yourself, is accessed with meditation. Be eager to recognize and receive all the help that is coming and see what happens! It can save you a lot of pain, suffering and trouble.

Finally, consider taking action on the information, aid, thoughts and ideas that come. It is in *doing* that you are freed from your prisons (self-imposed, obligatory, or outside influenced). A word of caution: Watch that you don't go overboard when first getting in touch with yourself. It *can* become a means to avoiding responsibility for your choices. Use discernment when committing to action, as you are ultimately responsible for all choices and outcomes in your life.

*You gain strength, courage and confidence by every experience in which you really stop to look fear in the face . . . . You must do the thing which you think you cannot do. ~ Eleanor Roosevelt*

*"Each time we face our fear, we gain strength, courage, and confidence in the* doing.*" ~ Source Unknown*

Consider the word FEAR to be an acronym for

> Fantasized
> Experiences
> *Appearing*
> Realistic

You can also do away with fear and limiting beliefs by infusing some passion into your life.

PASSION can be thought of as

**P**owerful
**A**ttitudes
**S**ustain
**S**ensational
**I**nspirations,
**O**utstandingly
**N**oteworthy

*"Each one of us has a fire in our heart for something. It's our goal in life to find it and to keep it lit."*—*Mary Lou Retton*

Strategies to triumph over fears are found in numerous good books, good people and good organizations.

*"There are two basic motivating forces: fear and love. When we are afraid, we armour ourselves and pull back from life. When we are in love, we engage with life with acceptance, openness and passion.*

*We need to learn to love ourselves first, in all our glory and our imperfections. If we cannot love ourselves, we cannot fully open to our ability to love others. Nor can we fully access our potential to create. All hopes for a better world rest in the open-hearted vision of people who embrace life with passion!"* ~ *Wayne Lee*

Suffice it to say that positive strong attitudes and beliefs, trust, faith and the biggie, love of self, are the anchors, the raw truth and the beginning of your journey to success.

*"And as we let our own light shine, we unconsciously give other people permission to do the same. As we're liberated from our own fear, our presence automatically liberates others . . ."* ~ *Nelson Mandela*

**L**ooking
**O**utward.
**V**aluing
**E**veryone.

**O**pportunities
**F**lowing

**S**ource
**E**nergy
**L**ovingly
**F**abricated

*     *     *

This chapter struck a particular chord in Kelly. She took
time to re-read some of the parts that she starred with her pencil.
It was as if this little manuscript was written just for her. This
particular section on fear resonated with Kelly right down to her
very core. Thinking back on the past few years of her life, Kelly
could now clearly see the small things that had accumulated into
larger and more substantial ways of being that slowly, but surely,
imprisoned her.

"What a lovely cage you've created for yourself, girlie," thought
Kelly to herself. Then it came to her that she was always a little
claustrophobic. She smiled and then laughed at the absurdity
of self-imprisoning herself when she knew how much she really
disliked tight, closed spaces. As she laughed even more, tears
started to well up in her hazel eyes. The more she laughed, the
more she cried. The harder she laughed, the harder she cried
until she ceased laughing altogether and just cried and cried and
cried.

At first, she couldn't imagine what had come over her. What
had caused such an odd reaction? Then Kelly got real with herself.

She knew *why* she wept so deeply. It was a cathartic release. The Truth had hit her hard right between the eyes. For once in her life, she had admitted to herself that she was responsible for what happened to her. She alone was the one who had locked herself inside of that invisible prison. She cried because the truth hurt. She cried because she felt sorry for herself and she cried because she was finally on her way to being set free.

Kelly was relieved that all the little and big lies that she had told to pacify herself, had come to an end. Yes! This was an end of an old former self and a beginning of a new Kelly. The release had lightened her load. She felt physically lighter, mentally more alert, emotionally more capable and spiritually freer. "The truth has set me free." "Oh brother!" thought Kelly. "Clichés coming out of the wood work too?" She laughed a more joyful laugh and then she gave a huge sigh of relief and release. Only one small tear remained in her right eye. Kelly smiled as she brushed away that last bit of moisture. Now it was time to get real and get to work.

# Eleven

# Dreaming and Planning and Scheming; Oh My!

*Love of Self—Step Towards Your Success*
    Chapter 10 So, Are You Happy Just Sitting on the Curb?
        Come Take a Walk with Me.

*"Standing on the corner watching all the girls go by." ~ The Four Lads-1956*

When you were young, this may have been a very acceptable and pleasurable way to spend your time. As adults, however, watching the girls or the world go by is not as fulfilling as it once was. Spending a few days dreaming about your hopes, wishes and dreams does play a part in your success and an important part at that. But it is a small role requiring only minutes, hours or a few days at most to fulfill its part of the process.

*"I like dreaming, 'cause dreaming can make you mine . . . ." ~ Kenny Nolan*

*Dreaming* is the first step to take when looking at your wish list. Dreaming allows you the time you need to consolidate the thoughts in your head and make a decision to pursue that goal. All, or at least most of the inspiration, can be first thoughtfully considered. For example, it may be a great idea to make a two row corn harvesting machine if currently only a one row corn harvesting machine exists. The time to do the job would be literally cut in half! Farmers could then spend more time with their families. Farmhands could be doing more enjoyable tasks if they did not have to spend so much time with the old one row corn pickers. It would indeed be a great time-saving, back-saving fantastic product to have!

Now, step two is at hand. After some great thought, some small simple steps or *some actions* are now required. In this illustration, perhaps in the form of a drawing or two, I decide to go to the *John Deere Tractor Company* with the idea (either on line or in person). In doing so, I discovered that not only are one row corn pickers obsolete, but that ten row corn harvesting machines are now being made. Furthermore, ten row corn pickers are as large a machine as the John Deere company is willing to make as their chassis are only capable of becoming a certain size while remaining affordable and practical. Well, so much for that great idea!

Actually, it's okay to have had that great idea. Really! Dreaming allowed me to think of other grand thoughts and be excited about something new. Taking a small action in the direction of fulfilling the first dream furnished me with several contact names for the next possible great invention—the "Whatchamacallit 2200". Now there's an invention worth dreaming about! Even the sales reps at the tractor company had implied that if someone would be able to solve the "extractor factor" dilemma that faces farmers world wide, they would certainly be willing to make a machine like that!

Almost instantly, I can see the design formulating in my head. I can feel the gratitude of the farmers across the globe as they quickly and easily put my great invention to work. The prices of the produce goes down, the corners on the mouths of the human race go up as they see their grocery bills are far less than they have ever been in a long time. I am so "pumped" thinking about all the people that would be happy because I took the time to dare to dream, took some steps necessary towards its fruition and focused on the big picture of serving my fellow man with an idea I just had received in my head. Wow! And most amazing of all, I get paid for having thought up this device! Isn't life just grand?

\* \* \*

Kelly furrowed her brow. Failure was not an option in her family's world. 'What ever you do you must do it well. Get it done right the first time. Measure thrice is good advice.' These and other such gems were what she grew up with. In fact, such sage advice was "responsible" for Kelly's "sensible" way of being. She was always known as the smart one, the responsible one, the one with a level head on her shoulders and the one that everyone could rely upon. Being first born, she had the eyes and ears of all the adults in her world, looking out for her well being. Everyone watched out for her—watched every step she took. She couldn't have made a mistake if she had tried. Her life was so different from Steve's.

By the time Steve came along, most of the adults and especially their parents had a different approach to child rearing. Being male may have also played some part in his rearing, but the bottom line was that Steve was his own person. And Kelly, well, Kelly was everybody's person. Kelly recalled being praised for her sound decisions, yet Steve was admired for his bravery, for taking chances while still landing on his feet and for having a killer sense of humour.

If she was to just blindly follow this advice, it would mean that Kelly would have to rethink her entire way of being. It would mean taking risks that may not even pan out. It would also mean that she would have to get over a failure and try again. This did not sit well in safe and cautious "Kelly World". As much as the previous chapter resonated with her, Kelly was not prepared to give up her sound and proper ways. She had lead a perfectly exemplary way of life. She took pride in that. It's absurd to just give that up and take risks, take chances, take a new direction in life. Yet, with this new information rattling around in her head Kelly had new options to consider. She could either keep doing what she has been doing ending up in known and predictable situations, or she could opt to take a step towards the unknown and change her life in new and wonderful ways that she had never entertained before.

Kelly thumbed through the little book, re-reading the starred and underlined areas. She realized that she really didn't have to actually physically do anything right now; she could just choose to think a little bit better about herself. Perhaps she could do that. It wouldn't be so bad to think a little more highly of herself; maybe even love herself, would it? Who would be hurt by her loving herself? Who could benefit from her loving herself? Besides, if she ever felt like it, she could change the world or at least her little corner of it, at some future date.

With that new thought and point of view in her mind, Kelly thought of Tim and Steve and of all the compliments and kind words they would say to her. In the past, she had always dismissed them, feeling rather embarrassed or unworthy or some other such emotion. People who love you are supposed to say nice things and be supportive. What they say isn't really what they mean and if it is, then it shouldn't go to one's head.

Well, that was in the past. Such down and harsh thinking has toughened her up, but at what cost? What is the benefit of *deflecting love* from others? Nothing. With a new resolve, she decided to think about her newest option. Perhaps if she accepted some of those words into her mind and being, that it would be a step towards loving herself. Kelly both admired and trusted these men. Both Steve and Tim would serve as a great reserve and well of love from which to draw upon.

Kelly reflected on how fortunate she was to have such a support system in her life. She hoped that others had someone's love and kindness to draw upon. She began to think of all of the people in her life who had touched her in a positive way. Images of faces filled her mind. There were teachers, friends, co-workers and family members. There were acquaintances, hairdressers, grocery people and bus drivers. There were neighbours, clergy, coaches and policemen. There were even waiters and waitresses at small obscure diners. A warm smile came across her face as Kelly remembered the two odd yet lovely people from Universal Delights. Indeed, she was a lucky lady to have so many people showing her kindness and love in one form or another.

What time was it? Almost two! Yikes! Well, no matter how interesting this book was, she had to get some running around done and it wasn't getting done sitting around. She resolved to get her tasks done quickly so that more time could be spent reading her new inspiration. With few commitments for this particular weekend, Kelly had a lot of free time to spend on herself. She felt happy to think that way. It felt kind of nice to be able to be a little self-indulgent; a kindness to herself. "Well, thinking warm fuzzy thoughts are not getting my errands done," she said aloud. Kelly got dressed, petted Charlie on the head and headed out the door.

As she set about completing her tasks, Kelly's mind remained fixated on the new information that she had acquired. Feelings of confidence, happiness and hope filled her being. From her mental wish list, Kelly picked out something that she wanted to make manifest. She dared to dream it into existence. Fueled by her interest and inspired inspiration, she dreamed up all sorts of possible (and some implausible) ideas.

As she brainstormed, she kept mental notes of the ideas that she received. Kelly thought of things that had never crossed her mind before. She wondered where some of these ideas came from. She felt almost as if she was being fed the information.

As Kelly went about completing her tasks, she noticed that there were a good number of ideas that related well to each other. They fit together. Mentally, she grouped these together and saw a plan emerge that could make this particular dream actualize.

In amongst all of those ideas, Kelly realized that there were some steps that she could take. Her wish and dream was forming into plausible plans. The plans were offering ideas for some small steps that she could take. Kelly was amazed at how fast it all came together. Spending some focused time daydreaming and thinking about a dream rewarded her efforts with ideas and plans for action. With her last errand complete, Kelly returned home to learn more.

# Twelve

## What Do You *Wish* To Attract?

*Love of Self—Step Towards Your Success*
   Chapter 11 Co-Creating

Wishing, dreaming, thinking and day dreaming lead you to the discovery of your desires and passions. Your thoughts have packets of energy that start the process of the Law of Attraction. It's your passions and desires that put the Law of Attraction into overdrive speeding towards you and leads to the creation of your realities. Doing what you love, are passionate about or happily desire, coupled with some action, is a great recipe for creating what you want.

Taking action, no matter how small, towards the dream or goal coming into being, alerts Spirit and your higher selves that you are serious about your intent to bring them into manifestation. It's the action—inspired action and commitment towards the end result, that enable you to take the dreams in your head out into the world at large. Inspiration and dedication will carry you through to completion.

The Universe does not take concentrated action on a wish list. Spirit understands commitment, as then It realizes that you are serious about your ideas and will rearrange Itself to accommodate you. In other words, the Universe will take care of the details, the *how*, the way that is the best for manifestation, for you.

There is no need to fear the outcome or to fear the Universe or God for that matter. Your dreams are *facilitated* by Spirit—co-created, if you will. The dream is not *done* for you nor is it handed to you on a silver platter. Together, the Universe *and you*, make manifestation possible. Then, both the Universe and you can experience what it is like to have that dream become reality.

One thing to note is the difference in both the feelings and the emotions between wanting something and needing something. There are occasions when you feel you absolutely need something to happen and there are feelings of sadness, anger, resentment or desperation attached to them. At times these needs are met, but at times they become elusive. Feelings of sadness, anger, resentment and desperation often push away or refract what you need. The *focus has changed* from the item or situation wanted and needed to the negative emotions and the drama of the whole situation. The new focus is what you receive more of—the Law of Attraction is working, just *not* to your benefit.

In contrast, the feelings behind what you want or desire contain fewer negative emotions behind them. Needs are defined as things that keep you alive: food, clothing, shelter, water, air, warmth, love and companionship. Without just one of these items, your very life is at risk, sometimes to the point of death. Wants, defined as items that would enhance your existence, have a lesser connotation, are less desperate in nature, and in fact, are often more optimistic in nature. Therefore, there is a greater chance of what is desired or wanted being acquired.

To illustrate, think of a person who is always in need of something or other. He can't catch a break. It seems that he goes from one desperate situation to another one. Where is this person's focus? It's usually on the plight of his situation, not on the actual happy end result. Compare this to some one who has an abundance of what ever is wanted and yet, receives even more. The focus is on the happily anticipated arrival of the item or end result. To coin a Ron Popeil phrase, "*Set it and forget it.*"

It's not, out of sight, out of mind, but rather, set your desire upon a specific outcome. Do not fret about how it will arrive, if it will arrive, when it will arrive or has it arrived yet?!? Keep the dream, idea, passion and want in mind, but never worry about its arrival. The doing part, the action part, the inspired action part are often minimal in nature, for example, talking to a key person or two, writing a letter, organizing a get together for a think tank, or making a drawing. The rest is taken care of for you in co-creation. It's just a slight change in focus and emotion that can bring about all the difference in the world.

*"The best and most beautiful things in the world cannot be seen nor touched . . . but are felt in the heart"*—Helen Keller

If you go within yourself, you are able to find your spirit there. Your spirit or God is invisible—unseen by the naked eye. It is invisible so that you are able to see the congruencies coming into your life to facilitate and co-create your own dreams. However, just like the wind, you see and feel the effects of its presence. It appears in many different forms in many different things, people, thoughts, ideas and inspired actions. The signs are given and all you have to do is pay attention.

Listen to the next song, ad on t.v., conversation, book and so on for clues to guide you to the next experience and act upon the information procured. You are never truly alone; you are part of a collective; you are one with God, Universe and All That Is. You have an infinite amount and supply of support and resources. All you need to do is listen, pay attention, be still, go within and trust that you will receive what you need. It's all there.

So, set it, forget it, but be mindful and open to what comes your way. When opportunity knocks, answer the door and *receive* it. Being *grateful* for its arrival is not necessary, but it does set you up for faster arrival of the next one. It's sort of like tipping the waiter up front. It provides for the opportunity for better service. Liking what is received makes for happy anticipation of the next item. Since there is already a happy memory of receiving in place, a positive pattern of acquiring what is wanted is being established. You are setting up a cycle of happily getting what is desired; a small yet easy thing to do with massive possible outcomes!

*    *    *

Kelly had heard about the Law of Attraction. She had read a few books that made mention of it. Her sister-in-law had spoken of it many times. Kelly recalled her discussion with Marla about the Law of Attraction. Focusing on what is both wanted and desired plays a large part. Countless Law of Attraction books clearly emphasize to focus on what you want rather than what you don't want. (Some worry that focusing on what you want places you in a state of want. If you are of that belief and/or opinion, use the words desire, wish, aspire, opt, pick, claim, select, intend or choose.) What you focus upon expands and attracts more of the same. You are vibrating most strong at that frequency at that moment. Whether you focus upon a like or a dislike makes no difference; you are operating and attracting things that are at that same frequency.

People constantly sort out preferences, likes, dislikes and the like, Kelly recalled. A subconscious knee jerk reaction such as a wince may demonstrate a dislike for vanilla; a smile, raised eyebrows and enlarged pupils shows a desire for the chocolate ice-cream. Since the people probably didn't dwell or focus on not getting vanilla and instead focused on acquiring chocolate, chances are they received chocolate ice-cream.

Another example the two had talked about revolved around driving. While driving through a speed trap some people may think, "Man, I'm glad I was driving at or around the speed limit. I think I'll be okay and be able to keep on driving." Seldom would they have been pulled over or had their licence plates photographed. Other people driving through a speed trap think, "Geez, another speed trap! Was I over the limit? Nah! Ooh, maybe I was. Darn it. I'll probably get a ticket. I hope I don't get a ticket. I don't want a ticket. I can't afford to pay for another ticket. Did the camera flash on my licence plate?"

Marla explained that in this example, the focus was on the "the ticket" . . . getting one, not getting one, not wanting one and other negative focused thoughts on "the ticket". "Does it really come as a surprise when their thoughts and feelings are so fine tuned into the frequency of 'the ticket' that they receive 'the ticket?' Not only were they tuned into 'the ticket' frequency with their focused thoughts, but the volume was up so loud with feelings of dread for 'the ticket', that it would have been a *miracle* had they *not* received it," Marla had said. Kelly had recalled having had similar thoughts once, yet miraculously, had not received a ticket. "Apparently miracles do happen," she thought.

Marla said that people may not exactly be going about their lives thinking, "I don't want that," but unfortunately they do *often focus in on the negative*; what's wrong, what's not going right; and how bugged they are feeling about those things. They tune into that frequency, boost the power and crank up the volume! "The Law of Attraction must give them what they have lasered their thinking and feelings upon," said Marla with her eyebrows raised and a grin on her face.

"Coming from a point of fear, anger, or even indifference does not serve people in any way. Where the attention goes, energy flows," Marla shared. Kelly figured that it would be better to let her attention flow toward what she wanted and desired and that served her in positive ways; to laser the flow, focus and feelings on an anticipated outcome, as if she already had received it. She hoped that she could bring that to life and into existence for herself.

Marla was into that metaphysical stuff. She was an upbeat person who enjoyed her life and all that it had to offer. She easily rolled with the punches and with Steve by her side, seemed invincible. Kelly sometimes envied her brother's wife but her love of this woman far outweighed any feelings of jealously. The two women had always got along and Marla seemed to make Steve happy and often amused. That is what mattered most to Kelly. She may not always have agreed with Marla's ways of doing things, yet if Steve was happy, then Kelly was happy. Marla made a fun addition to the family.

Kelly wondered if the happy couple had attracted each other through the Law of Attraction. Both had shared with Kelly that each had found what they were looking for. Neither had ever mentioned about being worried that they would never find the love of their lives. It is where you focus your attention that comes more clearly into view.

*     *     *

Kelly thought of how she and Tim had met. She was ready to settle down and was looking for a special man to show her his love. She did get what she wanted. Tim was an expert at showing Kelly just how much he loved her in ways that meant something to her; in her "Love Language" (The Five Love Languages ~ Gary Chapman). Although he was an affectionate man, he respected her wishes of few public displays of affection. Behind closed doors, Kelly felt safe and could share her love for him more freely. Tim enjoyed the special attention he received.

Occasionally Kelly had wondered if there was something missing from their relationship. She could never put her finger on it, but every now and then she felt like something was missing. She wanted something more, but more of what, she did not know. She saw how happy Steve and Marla were and definitely wanted a loving relationship like theirs, but did not want to rock the boat, so to speak, with Tim. Who else could love her like he did? No one. Kelly was sure of that. Yet, each person demonstrates love in their own unique way. Who is to say which demonstrations of love are right for a person except for that person? Who is to say that another person could not love you just as much but in a different manner?

Kelly missed Tim. She missed his strong arms around her. She missed that loving sense of peace and security. She missed her pal and confidant. Kelly wondered if the feeling of being loved, the feeling of peace and the feeling of security were almost more important than her relationship with Tim. How a person feels around another person is what attracts or repels them one from another. Combining that with the primal urge to pair up, is what often gets people united. Deciding to love that person for a long time often commits the people to staying together.

Kelly wondered if there was a higher potential for relationships between people. Perhaps she would think on that thought a little later. Right now, her eyes needed a break from reading and her brain wanted to stop thinking about this topic, if only for a little while. Kelly put down the book and prepared a cup of tea for herself and got out some catnip for Charlie.

# Thirteen

## Shoes

*Love of Self—Step Towards Your Success*
Chapter 12 What a Selfish Thought!

In his book Secrets of Closing the Sale, Zig Ziglar said, "*You can get everything in life you want if you will just help enough other people get what they want.*" Ziglar's very popular quote is chosen by many to help sales people change their sales approach from selling from a selfish point of view to thinking about humanity's needs first. Then, through due course, they have their own needs realized. People love to buy but they don't like being sold.

This quote also supports looking after you in a *selfish* way as well. Remember that loving yourself leads to success which leads to others being served. When there is an intent to provide a service, product, course or a better mouse trap that will be of benefit to society, but you are unable to do so because you can't get over feeling too shy, scared or unworthy, then you are then of *no* service to anyone! You have not served or aided humanity to get what it wants. So, when you start by finding ways to nurture yourself and love yourself, then humanity at large get its needs met, thus enabling your own needs to be met.

*      *      *

Kelly found herself smirking as she finished reading the tiny chapter that packed a big punch. Two weeks ago, her boss asked her to give a brief presentation on an idea that she had shared with him, to the board of directors. Kelly had wanted to help shape the policies and programs that impact people in a positive way. She remembered how flattered she felt that he wanted her to present the idea and how terrified she was to speak in front of a group of people. After he started walking away from her desk she suddenly got up the nerve to protest his proposal, but he ignored her frantic opposition. He just kept walking away calling over his shoulder, "You can handle it. I have faith in you." She remembered thinking, 'But I have no faith in myself.' She had one week before the next board meeting to get her presentation in order.

Kelly had all the content already documented, so putting it into a presentable order would not take too long. It was the very thought of having to pitch an idea while not knocking her knees or fainting that had Kelly rattled. She had her power outfit picked out so that she would at least look like she belonged in the board room, but wanted an extra bit of a confidence booster to help seal the deal. And that's when it hit her—shoes. She would buy a stunning new pair of shoes to complete her ensemble.

Like most women in the work force, Kelly had a few too many shoes already. Tim would lovingly tease her about the closet full that she already possessed when ever she came home with a new pair. It was her one 'vice'. She didn't smoke, drink, do drugs, sleep around, buy expensive jewellery or collect a myriad of knick-knacks, but she did buy shoes. Why? It made her feel good about herself. She felt it was very important to feel good from the ground up; to have a firm foundation upon which to stand. If she felt good in her shoes, she felt she could accomplish most any task.

Kelly had always felt a little self-indulgent, a little selfish to have so many shoes. She had thought of ways to justify to herself the reasons why she was buying the newest acquisition. Ultimately, however, she knew that deep down inside she just felt great in her new shoes. It was a little like purchasing a bit of confidence. It worked for her. It was a way that she looked after her needs. It was a way to share a little bit of love with herself; that she was *worthy* of this *investment* in *herself.*

When the day came for Kelly to give her presentation, she felt she looked the part of a successful presenter. The company was looking for ways to be more eco friendly—more of a conscious corporation—to please the share holders. Several bosses of various departments had posed various options to consider. Kelly's boss introduced her and she was on her own.

Kelly shared her information on what some companies on the pulse of the planet are doing from an eco and a conservation point of view. She showed her data on how the company could take direct action into saving wildlife habitats by purchasing land which would become permanent wildlife reserves. The local people would benefit by becoming hired employees who looked after the land. With jobs created, species preserved and the company benefiting from the good standing from both the shareholders and the public at large, Kelly felt that she had presented a sound idea that held merit. Her boss thought so too and had told her so.

Kelly had felt honoured, elated and very conscious of how much the company and the world at large would benefit from such actions. Being selfish, showing herself a little love and standing in the footsteps of Zig Ziglar, so to speak, could one day benefit the whole planet in some way. Kelly had realized her higher potential for that period of time.

# Fourteen

## Who's In Command Of Your Ship?

*Love of Self—Step Towards Your Success*
Chapter 13 Does Life Feel Like a Roller Coaster Ride?

Are you happy? Do you even know what brings you joy? What makes you smile, or make your eyes light up? What makes your heart sing? How long do you sustain feelings of happiness? Do you dwell upon the joyful times and remember them often? Do you frown more than you smile? Are you satisfied with *anything* in your life? Why? Why not? What are your predominant thoughts? Are they of a positive or negative nature?

When was the last time you had a good belly laugh? Who was with you when that happened? Where were you when it occurred? What were the circumstances that lead to that happy time? Why was it so funny that you had to almost hold your sides from splitting? How can you replicate that time again? Is it good enough to just be immersed in the memory or do you need to get out and get together with others to recreate that feeling again? Think about it. Really think about it.

People tend to be creatures of habit. You will often do things in a habituated manner and run on auto pilot, coasting through your lives. Only when things start to go astray do you wake up and take notice; it may come in the form of an accident, an illness of a close relative, or your own mental, emotional or physical being changing in a negative manner.

Anything that happens to you first happens in your ethers (the place just outside of yourself where your soul lives), before that thing comes to you in a physical form. You may find this difficult to believe, but let's imagine for now that this is true. In this context, let's say that a person had developed cancer. There's now a huge amount of scientific evidence to support the notion that the cancer "switch" was turned on. Further, that the majority of these cancer cases happened to people who were predominately unhappy, experienced a lot of stress or felt disempowered prior to their diagnosis.

You are aware of people who have succumbed to accepting cancer as a death sentence and have died a short while after being told. You are also aware of people who have changed what they thought and did and fully recovered. And further aware of some who have returned to health without any medical support at all! What happened in these cases first started from *habituated* ways of thinking, behaving and especially *feeling*. What happened afterwards resulted from either a *continuance* of same thinking and feeling or a *change* in thinking, behaving and feeling.

Let's consider what could make people fall into depression. Again, let's imagine that what you think, do and feel happens first out in the ethers before it comes to a physical state in your bodies. You are running on autopilot and things seem to be going fairly well. Then, you start to notice that you don't feel the same amount of joy that you used to feel. Things that used to bring you pleasure or a smile to your faces don't seem to have the same impact that they once did. You analyze it and postulate that your tastes have changed, you are maturing, or it's just the blues. In some cases, you bounce back because you have distracted yourself from the negative and focused on the positive.

In some cases though, you dwell upon the negative and start making *that* a new habit. You were a fairly happy person before, and most who know you would still see that in you, but now what you show on the outside as a habitual façade does not really demonstrate your new feelings. You look for validation from others as to how you are truly feeling and they say you seem just fine. But you know different. Things are not fine. They haven't been for some time now. Life goes on and you manage as best as you can, but it seems to be more effort than it was before to keep up the façade.

Soon enough, those close to you begin to take notice and may comment on it. Next thing you're in the doctor's office and have been prescribed therapy and/or medication to cope with the new condition. Here too, scientific evidence supports that negative thoughts and feelings have lead to a state of depression. Once again, you have the choice to focus on health and bounce back to life or continue with the negative thoughts and have to rely solely on medication to alter your mood.

What ever the diagnosis is, getting the help that you need, in other words *taking action*, be it medical, wholistic or will power, is the first step towards a successful recovery. Once you feel you are more in control of your minds, feelings and emotions (you have a choice as to how you react to any given situation), you are able to formulate more rational decisions to make yourself happy, healthy and productive once more.

When you *stop* looking at all the reasons why something will not work then you start healing. Good health is yours for the taking. Take some positive action towards it and know that it is yours to claim. You have to make the choice yourself. Seldom will outside influences and good intentions from others be enough to for you to fully succeed. *You* are the deciding factor in your health, happiness and success in your life; no one or *nothing else*—just you.

The following poem is often used to convey a powerful message. Too often people dismiss this sage piece of advice as it has become part of the pattern of the wallpaper of their lives. Read it once more and consider the information that it provides.

### Serenity Prayer

*God grant me the serenity*
*to accept the things I cannot change;*
*courage to change the things I can;*
*and wisdom to know the difference.*
*Living one day at a time;*
*Enjoying one moment at a time;*
*Accepting hardships as the pathway to peace;*
*Taking, as He did, this sinful world*
*as it is, not as I would have it;*
*Trusting that He will make all things right*
*if I surrender to His Will;*
*That I may be reasonably happy in this life*
*and supremely happy with Him*
*Forever in the next.*
*Amen.*

*~ Reinhold Niebuhr*

What does it mean? Written by Reinhold Niebuhr in 1943, these words often hold special meaning to people seeking solace during times of turmoil, despair or uncertainty. What this piece suggests is, be aware that in whatever circumstances you find yourself, trust that you have the *solution* within to overcome any situation.

It further illustrates that you will come across trials in your lives. By not fighting or being angered by the circumstances, but rather accepting them as part of life, you are better prepared to deal with them and move on. It is a smart and balanced way of dealing with life.

It also intimates that there are things in place to facilitate your triumph. Continually remembering to focus on the good times each day, one day at a time, brings you peace, happiness and success in life. A regular thought or a prayer that promotes wisdom or guidance is also a good practice. Thinking, doing and behaving in manners that are often positive in nature and intent, can lead to healthier and more fulfilling lives.

It's important to keep your sights on your wants, goals, intentions and desires. Being optimistic allows for greater freedom to accomplish that task; where as being pessimistic allows for barriers to block vision of your goals.

Blocked vision, lack of knowledge, problems, destroyed dreams and certain emotional patterns can make you ill. Negative repetitive thoughts and patterns cause a type of brain fog. Repressing your own needs while looking exclusively after the needs of another is conducive to being emotionally isolated (suppresses the immune system). Being an exclusively positive thinker often leads to self-suppression which also suppresses the immune system.

You are out of balance when you suppress and bottle up fear, anger, sadness and negative emotions. *Expressing healthy* anger, grief, loss, sorrow, sadness, disappointment, fear and negative emotions allows you to let go of that which does not serve you and weighs you down. It allows you to keep your balance, your health and your sanity.

The main key to staying in command of your own ship is to be in balance of your own life. (Become the pilot—steer and control your own destiny; couple that with poise and equilibrium.) Have a healthy mindset. Being aware of your habituated ways of thinking, being, doing and feelings allows you to correct and continue your life in balance. Being balanced in life is the firm foundation that you build upon strong and successful ways of thinking, being, doing and feeling.

You set yourself up for success by having beliefs and intentions that are realistic. Consider the following set of examples.

| *Unrealistic* | *Realistic* |
|---|---|
| 1. To always be comfortable and feel happy about myself and my life. | 1. To accept the reward and success that some patience and personal effort offers. |
| 2. To always have fun and never be bored. | 2. To enjoy life and be creative during boring and tedious times. |
| 3. To avoid competition (to avoid experiencing fear, loss, failure, problems and disappointment). | 3. To strive for and reward personal best (accepts that competition is part of the real world (be it against others or against self); learns how to successfully deal with fear, loss, failure, problems and disappointment thus building resilience and self-esteem). |

When you put in effort (of any form) you are far less likely to exhibit or have signs of depression than people who've had things handed to them. (The victory is sweet when the win requires effort. Most any athlete or competitor will attest to that!) Cheerful people have more endorphins in their system. Endorphins make you happy. Happy balanced people seldom get ill. Work to get better at things. It's the effort that gives you satisfaction and builds that sense of self and success.

*   *   *

Kelly drank her tea and read the Serenity Prayer once more. Then she thought back to the barrage of questions asked at the beginning of the chapter. Her mind filled with these questions and more. Was she operating on autopilot? She hoped not, but feared that that was indeed the case. She had once heard on one of the alternative radio talk shows to stop choosing the same potentials or choices as you have done for eons of time. Instead of being caught up in the situations, go with your desires and passions. Things that you desire or are passionate about are what the soul aspires to do. In doing so, you are able to realize your higher potentials.

The host of *Healing With the Masters,* Jennifer McLean, was interviewing Dee Wallace. During that time, Kelly recalled, Dee Wallace assisted in clearing a caller's problem. Ms Wallace told the audience about how patterns of behaviour were being brought to her attention. She was advised to tell her audience to break the patterns of ancestral Karma and drama that were plaguing people.

Kelly wondered if by following passions and desires, (things which make you happy and bring you joy) that she would avoid many of the negative emotions that could potentially lead to diseases and low feelings. Dis-ease; the body is not at ease. Illnesses often show up in bodies that are not at ease; it's been well documented by a variety of sources, traditional, wholistic, alternative and other means. She had learned a lot from Marla about the power of being positive. Kelly wasn't sure if what Marla said held water at the time, but here, now, after reading this chapter, she started to shift her thinking a little. Perhaps there was indeed something behind what Marla said.

Bringing her attention back to the group of questions, Kelly thought about her life being on auto pilot. Who was driving the ship? Where was the captain of the vessel to be found? If she was not in charge of steering herself, then who was? Just how efficient, safe and productive was it to be on auto pilot for an extended period of time? Kelly could see the benefits of being on auto pilot for a short period of time; it gives a person a break; it provides a chance to step back, reflect and regroup; it allows time to heal while doing what is necessary to get back on track. However, she could see many pitfalls to allowing others to command her ship, or perhaps even worse, no one watching and taking command of her ship. She could go astray and not even realize that she was off course. If she strayed often and for long periods of time, she could even end up in places that she never wanted to see, doing things she never, ever wanted to do.

What made her happy? At first she could not think of anything. Then Charlie pounced up onto her lap, startling Kelly. Yes, Charlie made her happy. She enjoyed his antics and his company. Then more thoughts of happy times came into her mind. As she thought about the people, events, things and yes, pets and companion animals with which she interacted, Kelly realized what it was that made her happy. It was the feeling of unconditional love and acceptance she received and the feeling of unlimited freedom that truly made her feel happy.

At the end, Kelly concluded that while she may not be the happiest person on Earth, she was, by and large, a reservedly happy person and that was indeed *"a good thing,"* as Martha Stewart would say. It also meant, however, that there was room for improvement in her life. She made a decision to seriously consider what she could do to change her life. She decided that she did not want to end up bitter or sad. Kelly wanted to be vibrantly alive, healthy, active and happy.

One thing that she could do would be to imagine being in a state of unconditional love, acceptance and freedom each time she got out of bed in the morning. She could resound and vibrate these feelings first within and then, outside of her being. Kelly thought that tuning into the frequency of unconditional love, acceptance and freedom, like tuning into a radio or TV station, would be an easy way to begin a new way of thinking. It would be a thought that she could have running in the back of her mind—like a computer that has programs running in the background enabling the smooth operation of the forefront applications or a song that keeps popping to mind. She liked the idea of starting off her day on the right foot and in the process, sending out and then drawing in positive, empowering, joyful and wonderful experiences to her like a magnet . . . like attracting like.

She found the table of realistic and unrealistic goals to be particularly interesting. How many children and adults held tight to the unrealistic side? Avoiding "work", avoiding effort and avoiding the use of patience, is *not* the easy way out. Such thinking leads to problems and illness physically, mentally and emotionally. "That is just too high a price to pay for short term gain and fame," thought Kelly.

*"It's important to keep your sights on your wants, goals, intentions and desires. Being optimistic allows for greater freedom to accomplish that task."*

Kelly liked this line from the book. Having *freedom* to accomplish her tasks was much better than self-imprisonment. A famous and brave Canadian once said, *"The only limitations that we have are those that we impose on ourselves." ~ Terry Fox* She'd much rather put in some effort, stay in balance, enjoy life, build a strong sense of self and happily accept the success that it all brings.

A peaceful yet elated feeling engulfed her as she reflected on the material she had just read. Kelly took a breath and let the feeling sink deeply into her body. She decided to take a little break from her reading. "After all, I want to be in balance," said a smiling Kelly to herself.

# Fifteen

## Breaking Patterns

*Love of Self—Step Towards Your Success*
Chapter 14 How to Come off of Auto Pilot

So, at last you are beginning to accept that *a happy, healthy and balanced future lie in your own hands*. Good. Now you are able to intentionally direct your thoughts in such a way that you can create the conditions for a positive outcome. You can continue your evolution consistent with this new positive vibration. Such new thinking will enable you to manifest what you want more easily and it will be a healthier and happier expression of yourself. As a result, you will break your ties with the old where it no longer serves you. It will allow you to walk free from its effect. You have ceased selecting the same potentials that you have for years. You have decided to go with your desires and passions. You have broken patterns of personal and ancestral karma and drama. At first, it may not be so easy to stay upbeat, positive and balanced. However, staying balanced within your light and happiness is a discipline that you will come to learn and excel at doing.

What can you do to overcome running on auto pilot and change your habituated ways of living? Let's consider focusing on the process of willingly changing a single habit. Before you do, it's important to realize that any and all changes that you want to have in your life come down to first changing your thoughts.

*"All that you accomplish or fail to accomplish with your life is the direct result of your thoughts."* ~ James Allen

When you change your thoughts, you change your emotions, which in turn change your actions. Without first changing your thoughts, no changes in your actions can take place. Without changes in your actions, you are destined to keep everything the same as it currently is now. All changes start and end with *you* and *no one else*. So let's take the first steps in the direction of where you want to go.

A simple four step process can set you on the course that you may wish to take:

First:
Identify the habit or routine.

Secondly:
Ask yourself, "How does this habit or routine serve me?"

Now consider:
What or how does this habit or routine hold me back or harm me?

Then finally ponder:
What can I substitute this habit or routine with that will take me in the direction that I truly want to go?

Let's consider a common pattern that many people habitually and unthinkingly follow—the tendency of eating unhealthy munchies between meals or after supper. Whether you believe that you should not be eating in between meals or whether you are of the opinion that it is better to consume smaller amounts of food throughout the day, is not the focus of this discussion. The focus is on the fact that what ever you are doing is not producing the result that you desire, namely, attaining and maintaining a healthy body weight.

1. First:
   Identify the habit, routine or ritual.

   - Consuming unhealthy snacks in between planned meals.

2. Now ask:
   How does this habit, routine or ritual serve me?

   - It is a break from my work routine (like a coffee or cigarette break).
   - It calms my nerves to eat during those times.
   - It abates the hunger pangs I feel, especially when I am cutting down on calories.
   - It quells the desire for something sweet, salty, greasy, etc.
   - It makes me feel happy and satisfied
   - It's a thrill to think that I've done something "naughty" and it tastes so good.

3. Next consider:
   What or how does this habit, routine or ritual hold me back or harm me? This is the "*why*" you want to achieve a new way, direction or state of being.

   There are a few areas that could be considered such as:

   * Blame—not wanting to be or feel responsible for the conditions experienced.
   * Opinion of self—I'm incompetent; I've always been this way; This is who I am.

* Failure exaggerated—failures are mentally and/or emotionally overblown and practically given life through focus of attention, thus making even the thought of success feel unattainable, hopeless and predestined to failure.
* Doubt—fear and mistrust in one's own ability to succeed.
* Making mistakes becomes a big deal—feeling frustrated, angered, flustered, scrutinized, victimized.
* Worry—a form of fear, focusing primarily on flaws and what could go wrong.
* Destructive attachments—negative feelings and associations to foods and tastes that are supportive toward achieving the goal.
* Constructive attachments—positive feelings and associations to foods and places that are unsupportive.
* Stress eater—using food to pacify or medicate.
* Too large of a job to tackle—unable to break down the tasks into smaller pieces.
* Calamity clamour—thinking of the worst possible scenarios.
* Physical indicators—feeling jittery, having digestive troubles, dis-eases, or sleeping disorders.

- I may be doing non-productive activities and wasting my time.
- I feel logy and bogged down after eating sugary or salty snacks.
- It exacerbates other conditions that I have or suspect that I may have.
- I actually feel depressed (not happy or satisfied) after eating empty-calorie foods.

- I feel badly that I've, yet again, gone off of my intended eating plan.
- My weight is not going in the direction I want it go.
- My weight is not near where I want it to be.
- My health is not as sound as it could be.

4. Then finally figure out: What can I do or substitute this habit or routine with that will take me in the direction that I truly want to go?

> \* I eat unhealthy snacks during unplanned times and yet want to continue on the road to success of releasing excess weight. The thought of having snacks in between planned meals rings strong with me.

- I could substitute unhealthy snacks with nutritionally sound snacks—snacks that are healthier than what I am currently eating.
- I am going to accept the fact that doing what I have been doing has not yielded the results I really do desire (attaining and maintaining a healthy weight).
- I am going to substitute my decision that I must snack in between meals with I must snack on healthy food and drink if I am going to snack in between meals.
- I am going to clean out the unhealthy snacks from work and home and replace them with healthy food that I like or will make up my mind to like.
- I am going to realize that since I reach for things out of habit; I will readily make available foods and drinks that are good for me to fill that void.
- I am going to remind myself of the Serenity Prayer or of any other thing that inspires me to stick to my plan

instead of putting myself down each time I experience a setback.

- I am going to focus on what I am doing right, instead of any errors in my judgement.
- I'll reward rather than punish myself.
- I'll consider replacing eating with an activity such as stretching, taking a quick walk, having a drink of water or calling a friend.
- Even better, I *am* replacing unhealthy snacking and eating with an activity such as stretching, taking a quick walk, having a drink of water or calling a friend.

A habit, routine or ritual is a small thought, gesture or mannerism that, over time, has created huge results. Altering or eliminating a habit that does not serve you is very empowering. You do not have to change your whole life in one grand motion. In fact, to do so may lead to failure and you may end up worse off for the grand attempt. Taking small steps in the direction of your dreams is realistic, productive and attainable and will afford you the greatest benefits.

*"Don't do great things, do small things greatly."* - *Mother Theresa*

Wise words indeed from a very insightful woman. Why should you focus on only a few things at a time? Your minds are practically designed this way. You seldom look at the big picture all of the time. In fact, most people focus on a small detail or series of small details. You first have a thought, then another and then another. Sometimes your thoughts focus on one thing, such as a flaw. Your next thought is often that you want that imperfection fixed. Sometimes that one small flaw ends up being the whole picture to some of you. You need to consider your perspective from several angles and substitute and/ or change some of the less desirable habits for ones that support you in the direction that you wish to go. Consistent small steps are your surest way to success.

Whether your habits, routines or rituals are physically, mentally or emotionally based, you have the power within you to have them serve your highest good. Access the part of you that is real and completes you. Ignore the part of you that is anesthetised. By looking at yourself and taking a moment to assess the quality of your habits, you are able to start the process of supporting yourself in positive ways. Your habits will become ways to get what you want.

Consider adopting this ten two-lettered word phrase: *if it is to be it is up to me.* Remember, of course that you are never truly alone in your efforts. When you focus and go in the direction of your desires, there is always assistance and guidance by nature of the Law of Attraction. Feelings of self-respect, confidence, happiness, fulfillment and satisfaction will ensue—guaranteed! Often you'll discover "*I like me*". You'll probably even love yourself a lot more for having put in the right efforts (as opposed to doing busy work that is non-productive towards your success). In fact, when looking back on the process, you'll probably find that there was more effort in the worry and resistance than there was in actually carrying out the tasks.

Why do people struggle so hard to *not* change their thoughts, attitudes, beliefs, word, actions and expectations? You are a funny and strange lot to figure out. Life is truly interesting.

*　　*　　*

*"Don't do great things, do small things greatly."* . . . *"If it is to be it is up to me."* . . . *"I like me."*

These thoughts repeated over and over in her head. Kelly went in search for her note book and an erasable pen. She wanted to work on a few of the ideas suggested. Although eating unhealthy snacks was not one of her areas that needed change, there were other areas that would benefit a change. Nail biting was a bad habit that she had tried to stop since her early teen years. Now it was an embarrassment to her when she ever would have to hand out material to people in her office. Another thing she wanted to get rid of was doubt. The book mentioned that doubt was a fear and mistrust in one's own ability to succeed. While it did not rule her, it certainly did play more of a major role in her life than she would ever want to admit.

After that thought, Kelly sort of hit a wall. It was as if her brain was overloaded. She had many, many, many things that she would like to change. She could picture them in her mind or catch fragments of the sentiments that she was thinking but not put them down on paper. "Whoa," thought Kelly. "I never thought that biting my nails was that big of a deal!" She laughed as she knew it was the issue of doubt that put her brain temporarily on hold. It felt good to be able to laugh at such a "bugaboo" of hers.

\*　　\*　　\*

In her laughter, Kelly released some of the attachment to her issues. She was in a positive vibration. She was in the process of letting go of that which no longer served.

Kelly was beginning to accept that she could construct a happy future. She had started the process of creating a positive outcome by directing her thoughts and creating the right conditions. Kelly wanted to start a *change* reaction in her life and had the right attitude to that end. There were no feelings of desperation that this task needed to be done. She was at choice—at the *cause* of the situation. With Kelly in this state of being, she easily employed the Law of Attraction and the Law of Abundance in her favour.

Had she been feeling guilty and berating herself for being in such a state, Kelly would be at the *effect* of her own negative emotions. She would not be in a position of positive power to make the changes that she desperately wanted to make. A focus with these negative emotions would only attract more negative energy. In this state, Kelly would experience the Law of Attraction (and perhaps the Law of Abundance), except that she would be on the "wrong" side of the Law.

# Sixteen

# A Written Assignment

*Love of Self—Step Towards Your Success*
Chapter 15 Set Your Sights: Aim High and Smile!

*"Think of every thought as a carefully selected arrow that you aim at a specific target and launch with expert control. And since no negative or contradictory thoughts clutter your mind, every thought sails unobstructed to instantly hit its target, returning the glory of its mark to you." ~ Ghalil pg. 37, Professional Dreamer*

"Have you had enough yet? Have you had enough?" Words to these effect started Neale Donald Walsch on his path to enlightenment and expression of his true self. The question is: Are you now at the point of wanting to make changes that are in alignment with your purpose, passions and true expressions of who you are? Have you had enough of the excuses and made up reasons that have held you back from doing, having and being everything that you want? Are you at the point where you are truly ready and wanting to take *truth* steps towards your magnificent life? Will you now consider looking at things that you were once too lazy or too scared to look at now? Really? Good! It's time you were passionate about you and your life.

*"Fear does not have any special power unless you empower it by submitting to it." ~ Les Brown*

Exchanging, changing or eliminating habits and rituals is one way of having, doing or being what ever you want in your life. There are other things to consider as well. Often, having some sort of desire for something more for your life is the very thing that sparks and sets you off on a new path of self discovery. So, let's get started!

*"You were born to win, but to be a winner you must plan to win, prepare to win and expect to win." ~ Zig Ziglar*

Pull out some paper and a pencil and begin mapping out some ideas. Draw a cloud in the center of the paper and put your name in it. Draw a circle or a heart in or around the cloud and put the word(s) "me" or "how do I love me; let me count the ways". Write words, draw pictures or symbols around this to illustrate ways you will show yourself self-love. Consider things like: listening to your inner voice, telling yourself that you are great, treating yourself like someone important, doing things for yourself that puts a smile on your face, finding your passion, discovering what makes you happy and what makes you laugh all the way up from your toes. If you have more concrete ideas, put them down too, such as: music, painting, salami sandwiches, dancing, fishing, resting against a tree, playing with the dog, bugging the cat, cooking, cleaning, drawing, intimate relations, talking to friends, skiing or singing. There should be a huge amount of ideas, pictures or icons on the paper by now.

New bubble: Great Ideas! Around this write, draw or scribble ways you will help yourself get pumped up and ways to sustain that enthusiasm. Consider: inspirational music, self-help books, tapes or videos, volunteering, joining causes that you care about, helping out your elderly neighbours, smiling, laughing, sharing great stories with friends and family, playing games, running, cycling, roller skating, swimming, chasing the dog, keeping a gratitude journal, writing a happy diary, walking in a mud puddle with your bare feet, counting the stars, taking a class or getting a different hair style.

New papers, new clouds: Chores/Goals/Dreams/Desires/ Have/Do/Be. Write them all down. List the "boring" ones like cleaning up the garage, declutter the bookshelf, rearranging the pantry, putting away all of the laundry or shoveling the sidewalk. Put down what you want to achieve such as learning a new language, live in a clean and tidy environment, wake up smiling or be more physically fit. Write out those things that you would never admit to others like learning "dirty dancing", take music lessons, sketch live models, recover from cancer or come out of the closet. Record the passions that you would love to pursue, your missions and your ideas.

More paper. Stop. Take a moment to consider the following categories: Spiritual, Mental, Physical, Emotional and Financial. From your previous pages, slot **one** of your thoughts into each of these categories. This is going to be your first set of tasks to accomplish. As each is achieved, cross it out and replace it with a new one. Please don't consider having 27 things going on at once. It's too much. Set your life with consciousness and intention. Focus. Don't multitask at this time. Remember, your focused and concentrated energy streams and efforts are more powerful, carry more oomph, and are completed more quickly if they are not fanned out over too wide an area. You may even want to keep track of all of the things that you've accomplished. Doing so in a journal may help keep you motivated, aware and on task.

*     *     *

Kelly set herself to task as described in the book. She felt warm and happy inside after seeing the list of things that made her life worth smiling about. She felt good about the mission. It gave her a bit of a boost. On a new paper, she wrote out the words chores, goals, dreams and desires. Under each of these categories she listed many ideas. The more she wrote, the bigger the smile on her face became.

Next, Kelly wrote out one word on each of five new papers. The words were Spiritual, Mental, Emotional, Physical and Financial. She looked back at the other papers to pick one item to put under each of these headings. Some were easy to choose, others took a little more time and consideration. Before too long, Kelly had her assignment completed and she finally took a break from writing.

The inspired writer took one last look over her list and then she went to get something to eat. Charlie followed in hot pursuit. It was time for his treat and he was not about to miss out on that. He usually interacted with Kelly a few times during the weekend days. Today, however, she had been so busy that he just played it cool (as only a cat can) and waited for a turn of events. "Meow! Purr. Mew. Mew. Meow!" Kelly looked with loving eyes at her charge. She bent down and stroked his body. Charlie arched his back when she got to the spot where his body met his tail. He loved having that particular area scratched.

"I guess I've been ignoring you, huh puss?' she said. Kelly reached for his special cat treats and placed 5 or 6 into a little dish. Charlie brushed by her legs one more time and then went to the dish. As the water boiled for tea, Kelly could feel her head swimming with thoughts and ideas of her latest task. She looked down at her watch. The time and the day had slipped by rather quickly.

The kettle whistled its tune and Kelly made herself a cup of tea. More thoughts and musings filled her head. She sipped her tea and grabbed an apple from the basket on the counter. As she headed into the living room, she thought about what she would do next. Knowing that she was near the end of the book, Kelly decided to read the remaining pages before tackling any more writing. Besides, she thought, her hand was a little sore from all of that activity. She gathered up all of her pages and placed them neatly into a pile. Picking up the book, she curled up on the sofa and set out to read once more.

# Seventeen

## Lessons Learned

*Love of Self—Step Towards Your Success*
    Chapter 16 So, What'll You Have, Do Or Be, Hon?

Something to Think About

By now, you have accomplished and created a great many pages of notes, have a head full of ideas and plans, and the determination to get the tasks underway and into production. Now stop for a moment and look at the big picture. You came across a little book that has taken you from curiosity, to thoughtful thought, to inspired action. You have a skeleton outline—a map of where you want to go and how you are to get there. Will you drive at mach 3 speed with your hair on fire? Perhaps you will take it at a slower pace and enjoy the ride. A blend of both would be a balanced approach.

Push through the more mechanical tasks and have fun and savour the other tasks. It is up to you as to what you have, do and be. You determine your own experiences. Yes, you must break through your addiction to drama and fear, but the bottom line is that you must look at the picture and determine what fits. Every time you make choices that are for your higher good, you see your life from a higher perspective. As you become more comfortable with change, you will more readily ease into the transitions. By looking at the possibilities instead of the fear or the difficulties you will see the opportunities for growth. There are important things that you and indeed, the world at large, will gain and benefit from your efforts.

To be sure, life is a self-fulfilling prophecy. Understand that fully. What you perceive will create all the reality you need to make it real for you. Now is the time to start looking for your passion and focus. What lights you up inside? What are your God given gifts; those unique expressions of God/Love/Universe within you?

Empower yourself first by taking as much responsibility for your own life as you can. It is going to mean shifting your own view of yourself a little. Here, responsibility is a good thing. Being responsible sets you free to enjoy the fruits of your labours. The more responsibilities you have, the more freedom and options you may explore. The fewer responsibilities you take on, the fewer choices you have and the more limited your freedom really is. Be responsible enough to yourself to go after what is in your heart and that will allow your spirit to shine through. Follow your heart and move in that direction, then everything will fall into place. Your responsibility is to share your gifts, talents, dreams, desires and your light in what ever way you *happily* and *comfortably* can. Every person *loses*—including yourself—when you do *not* share your light.

Ask, "How can I do this?" and then listen for the answers, look for the clues, accept the guidance and have the courage to take the first step. You can do it.

*I* believe in *YOU*.

\*    \*    \*

Kelly had tears in her eyes when she read those last few sentences. It felt as if her whole head, no, her mind had opened up to all the new possibilities that life had to offer. The more she stared at the last four words, the more her eyes welled up. Time and the Earth stood still for her for a short while. She was awestruck. She felt dumbstruck.

"Someone believes in me. Someone believes in *me*," she thought. She gave a huge sigh and smiled. She was glad she came across that little diner and in a sense, given a new lease on life.

# Eighteen

## And Your Choice Is . . . . ?

*Where you direct your thoughts is where your energy goes, and the more you focus upon it the stronger the link becomes for you. So you can see Dear Ones, why it is important to keep in your sight the beneficial changes . . . In so doing you are helping manifest them quicker than they might have done otherwise. Your present reality developed in this way and hence you say that you created it yourself.*

*. . . I have given you much to think about that will allow you to finish this cycle with complete happiness. ~ SaLuSa as channeled by Mike Quinsey*

Most people have a yearning to better themselves or their situations. The place to start in either case is *within* you. Take to heart the importance of loving yourself—being kind to you. When you love and respect yourself, then others will begin to do the same.

Then, take some comfortable steps toward something that you desire. Choose to make it a priority in your life. Know that the small amount of time spent is well worth the time and effort. It will very soon pay off.

*"Don't do great things, do small things greatly."*
*"If it is to be it is up to me."*
*"I like me."*

Let these words be of guidance and support. Once comfortable with doing small things greatly, then move on to larger scaled things. Get good at doing things greatly. Use your imagination, enthusiasm and positive power energy to accomplish your tasks. Before long, not only will you be sailing in the direction that you want, you'll *be* the Captain of your ship!

*"Achieve greatness through the power of a dream." ~ John Furlong, President of the Vancouver Olympic Committee, Vancouver 2010 Winter Olympics closing ceremony.*

One more thing to consider: personal responsibility. For some, such words mean having the weight of the world upon their shoulders. For others, it means a necessary evil. Some people spend their whole lives trying to avoid it at all costs. It is a full time job for them! A lot of time, effort, energy, excuses, more excuses, dodging and even more excuses are needed to successfully *avoid* taking on responsibility. In the end, it is simply not worth it. In avoidance, there is a build up of karma. At the end of it all, you'll have to work on the issue until it gets resolved. It's in your highest and best interest to take control and lead rather than to ignore and coast. The choice becomes to pay yourself now or pay yourself later. And your choice is . . . . ?

\*     \*     \*

Indulge me by reading the following and truly giving the words and their meaning a chance to resonate within your being before casting any judgement. There are two elementary students in a classroom who have asked to stay in for recess in order to finish a project. One of the students is quite high spirited. She is spontaneous, sneaky and has been known to look into other students' desks. A pleasant enough girl when she speaks to the teacher. She gets her work done on time and has a great sense of humour. However, when she walks past others on her way to or from the pencil sharpener she either stops to chat with them, says a snide comment or gets them to laugh at her antics. Her name can be seen written up on the board and occasionally she has to stay behind to chat with the teacher about her behaviour.

The second student is also somewhat high spirited, yet is often thought to be a good kid all around. She is considered to be a responsible girl. She looks after her belongings, hands in her work on time, looks after her needs in a careful manner and has proved herself to be trustworthy.

The teacher needs the recess time for a bathroom break and prep time for the next assignment. He knows that he'll be out of the classroom for a few minutes at a time. He wants to honour the girls' requests to complete their project. It is admirable for the students to want to be so accountable. However, he only allows one of the girls to stay in. The other girl is instructed to go outside to play. Which one did he allow to stay in?

Chances are you have chosen the second girl and you would be right. In the teacher's eyes, she is a responsible student whom he could trust to stay on task. Her reputation had been established and the teacher feels comfortable in granting her this rare request. It was because she had the reputation of being dependable that he allowed her stay in. She was granted that freedom and privilege because she had already proven herself to be responsible. In fact, had the second girl asked most any reasonable request, chances are she would have been granted it more often than not.

Such is true in the life of an adult. Think about it. You establish yourself as a person of trust and integrity. Chances are, if you were to approach your boss for a reasonable or even odd request, that you would be granted it. If, however, your negative reputation preceded you and you ask the same request, there's a good chance that your request would be denied.

The bottom line is responsible people are granted more opportunities and have more freedom. In a sense, they have earned the right for such privileges. What does the word responsible really mean? According to Dictionary.com, one meaning is [being] "capable of rational thought or action." This is the meaning that is intended in this writing. Wearing the mantle of personal responsibility means that you yourself hold yourself as a person able to think and act in a manner that is rational. Rational merely means sensible and reasonable. (ibid) So, really, being responsible is not scary or difficult. It simply is a way of being that is sensible and reasonable. It is having a reputation of being a good person.

*Opportunity is missed by most people because it is dressed up in overalls and looks like hard work. ~ Thomas Edison*

If you take on the mantel of responsibility and wear it well (as opposed to wearing it like an anchor around your neck) you have a great thing going. Never choose to view being responsible as a thing of weight, burden, gloom or a punishment. Take pride in being a responsible person. If you wish to take being responsible up a notch, then and only then consider being responsible for something outside of yourself. The more that you can responsibly handle; the more that you will be able and allowed to handle. It's the difference between being in the mail room or being the CEO of the company; in the boiler room or at the helm, captaining the ship. Which position would you rather be in?

Be honest with yourself. If being in the mail room is where you truly want to be, then that is great. It's where you should be. You know what you can handle. If, however, you wish for more, then accept more. That's right. Just *claim it* as yours and sooner or later it will be.

The little girl was granted her wish because she acted in a responsible manner. It was *not* because she was responsible for everyone and everything. Being responsible does not have to include taking on extra work or roles. It does not mean being a door mat for others to walk upon. Remember that like attracts like. Being responsible for everyone and everything attracts more of the same. If that is what you wish for yourself then fine, continue. However, the point here is to behave in a responsible manner—take responsibility for yourself, your feelings, your thoughts and your actions. Being trustworthy, honest, honourable and truthful is the way to freedom and better opportunities. Take one step at a time and you'll be on your way to the place, position or situation that you wish to *have, do or be.* Personal responsibility . . . what a concept!

*"To be, or not to be" ~ Shakespeare* Shakespeare's words need not only refer to life or death, although there certainly can be a feeling of life or of death in your present situation. Which feeling do you wish to have, do or be?

Have you decided to gain a higher state of awareness and consciousness? Do you seek answers to your *why?* Are you looking for a beginning to your path to understanding why life is not going as you had hoped and desired? Are you looking for a change?

Yes? Great! This means you are ready to do something about your life! You are here because you wish to start taking steps toward living your truth. Hooray! You will look at clearing your fear and then figure out what is wanted and desired. Then you can take some small consistent actions towards manifesting. You will soon be living your dreams and rejoicing in your accomplishments!

Reflect and enjoy making your life a dream come true. Start to shift and you will see everything in a new light. Guaranteed! Did you think: "But am I really ready?"

The very fact that you sought this knowledge proves that you were *wanting* to. You are *ready* to live a fulfilling life. This information will consistently find its way to all those who are prepared to live a different life than before. It was no accident that you found this book. There are no "accidents."

You *are* on your path to enlightenment. Make no more excuses. Accept no more excuses. Take on the mantle of responsibility and be **free** to have, do or be what ever you wish! In taking on this positive power, you have started a *change reaction* in both yourself and the world. A ripple effect that has already begun to affect the whole world in a wonderful way; all because you decided to love yourself enough to let your light shine. Don't hide yourself any longer. Not one minute longer.

*The world can not receive your gifts until you make a definite decision and act upon it . . . .*

*Express what you have bottled up inside of you.*

*We need you.*

# Author's Note

A note about the two workers in the diner:

The waitress and the cook who worked at the diner were worried when Kelly switched from a positive state to focusing negatively on her order. As the Law of Attraction personified, their role is to bring into existence what ever is focused upon.

Both the woman and the man knew that while a single thought or two were not enough to "switch" Kelly's order to what she *didn't* want. They did, however, know and understand that the more a person focuses on the down side, the more difficult it would be to turn it around. Thus instead of producing the original order, they would have to provide the one that matched Kelly's new frequency. The waitress and the cook were going to have to carry out their assigned tasks regardless of it being in Kelly's best interest or not. Kelly has free will and choice to make that decision as she pleases. Where her thoughts flow is where the energy will go.

# Sources Section

*www.TheAwareShow.com*

*www.HealingWithTheMasters.com*

*www.LightHeart.me*

*[1] (http://www.physicsclassroom.com/Class/newtlaws/u2l1a.cfm)*

*www.Dictionary.com*

# Soon to be Released

- Love of Self—Steps Towards Your Success, Workbook
- Love of Self—Steps Towards Your Success, Workbook, eBook version
- So, What'll You Have, Do or Be, Hon?—Living Your Truth, Loving Yourself, Changing Your Life and the World, eBook
- So, What'll You Have, Do or Be, Hon?—Living Your Truth, Loving Yourself, Changing Your Life and the World, audible book
- So, What'll You Have, Do or Be, Hon?—Living Your Truth, Loving Yourself, Changing Your Life and the World, audible eBook
- Love of Self—Steps Towards Your Success, Channeled Life Lessons
- Love of Self—Steps Towards Your Success, Tools for Transforming Your Life Courses.
- Versions of the above books in German
- Versions of the above books in French
- Versions of the above books in other languages

# About the Book

What if you decided to gain a higher state of awareness and consciousness?

Within this little book are transformational insights that are straightforward, easy to understand, inspiring to read and even fun to do. Revealed are ways to alter self-defeating patterns that have probably prevented you from enjoying your life for quite some time. Just imagine gaining back your physical or mental health, happiness, and even past successes. Envision having the future you always desired!

Huppertz's premier book offers down to earth advice that was channeled from Universal sources. *So, What'll You Have, Do or Be, Hon?—Living Your Truth, Loving Yourself, Changing Your Life and the World* is a story about a young woman and her thoughts on the information she reads in a book gifted to her. As she reads and reflects upon the material, she gains insights into herself and her world. Looking to understand why her life has not gone as she had hoped, the woman reads on and, as a result, gains a higher state of awareness and consciousness.

Follow along as Kelly reads and reacts to the information in a book given to her at a small diner called Universal Delights. A little book titled *Love of Self—Steps to Your Success* was placed under her food order. The intriguing title was the just the beginning of the journey that Kelly would take that weekend. Although not aware that a wish for something new would start an avalanche of love, information and support, and the assistance from the Law of Attraction in the form of two workers at a local diner, Kelly begins a process that answers her wish and her silent prayer.

Join Kelly in her choice of action to release what no longer serves and embrace the Truth presented. Enjoy her thoughts, reflections and reactions as she embarks on a journey to make her life a dream come true. Start to shift yourself as you begin to see a new and truthful light.

This information will consistently find its way to all those who are prepared to live a different life than before. Are you ready? Engage!

# About the Author

From a young age, Monika knew that she was different from her peers, often feeling that she stepped to the beat of a different drum. She always felt a unique connection to God. In her early twenties, she began to expand that connection into learning, adapting and utilizing various healing modalities. Now with over 25 years in the Spiritual and Alternative Health areas, she facilitates learning, living and experiencing positive growth in these fields. Monika has been open to channeled messages since 1998. In 2008, she received most of the information found in the pages of *So, What'll You Have, Do or Be, Hon?—Living Your Truth, Loving Yourself, Changing Your Life and the World*, her first published book. After honoring Divine timing, the balance of the material came flooding in and the book came into fruition.

The name Monika is of German descent and means advisor or counselor; from the Latin 'moneo' to advise, warn, counsel. She became a special needs teacher where her natural counseling abilities were an asset to her in her chosen profession. As her skills in the metaphysical region grew, inborn abilities emerged. It was her students who alerted Monika that she was ready to start sharing these gifts and talents with the world. Children who acquired "owies" on the playground sought out her "magic hands" to help make the hurt go away. Monika is currently teaching in an elementary school in Edmonton, Alberta, Canada.